Highs and Lows

This book is dedicated to the number one person in my life, my Gabe, and to my beautiful boy, Buster Llŷr, our golden retriever.

I wish to thank members of my beloved friendly Garden and BBC Wales, and in particular my BBC Radio Wales editor, Steve Austins, for the support and loyalty they've shown me over the years, especially through my serious illness.

Many thanks to my publisher, Lefi, at Y Lolfa, for his patience and understanding.

I honestly believe that without these incredible people I wouldn't be here today. I've always answered to my Lord and I thank him for giving me a second chance.

God bless you all
Chris

Highs and Lows

Chris Needs

First impression: 2013

The publishers wish to acknowledge the support of
Cyngor Llyfrau Cymru

Editor: Gabe Cameron

Cover design: Y Lolfa
Cover photograph: Simon Winkler

ISBN: 978 184771 377 3

Published and printed in Wales
on paper from well maintained forests by
Y Lolfa Cyf., Talybont, Ceredigion SY24 5HE
website www.ylolfa.com
e-mail ylolfa@ylolfa.com
tel 01970 832 304
fax 832 782

Foreword
by Gabe Cameron

I GUESS THAT threw you for a start! Bet you never thought you'd see my name at the top of the page. I've progressed from a mention on the back cover to penning the final chapter of Chris' last book, and now I've been asked to write the foreword to this, his fourth book. Maybe not so much a foreword, but more of an introduction. I suppose you could say that having been Chris' partner for almost half my life I might just be qualified. But then, to quote Margaret Rose, Chris' mother, "You can live with someone for 50 years and never truly know them," but that goes for all of us.

When Chris was originally asked to write his autobiography he insisted that he wanted to tell all, the whole truth, and leave nothing out, including the abuse he suffered which continued to torture him well into adulthood. He felt that the demons would be exorcised and he'd be finally able to get on with his life. Unfortunately, that wasn't to be and those revelations have continued to be the focus of his life.

Chris knew that the second volume of his autobiography, although equally well received, still had dark issues running through it. He has always maintained that he cannot keep up the pretence of being the 'court jester' 24 hours a day, but that doesn't make him a miserable person, just that he doesn't feel or want to be cracking jokes all the time. Chris had said that he needed to take a break before returning to writing and knew that any additional material would have to be much lighter to balance out his personality. He had numerous ideas, including the history of the 'Garden' which, at the time, was due to celebrate ten years; interviews with members and their recollections of meeting and making friends with each other, and featuring the numerous photographs they'd taken.

Chris was always most prolific at writing during the early hours once his radio show was over. It helped him relax and eased him to sleep – eventually!

During November 2010 Chris attended a diabetes clinic check-up. He'd previously been prescribed medication derived from simulated lizard's spit, as he referred to it. He was looking well, feeling good in himself and had been losing weight. Unfortunately, although the weight loss was noticeable, it wasn't significant enough as far as the consultant was concerned and Chris was prescribed additional medication. This proved to be detrimental to his general health.

What started out as a sore throat a few weeks later, which Chris initially attributed to a winter cold and was treated with a course of antibiotics, escalated into a series of ulcers. These spread from his gums and tongue to the lips, nasal passages, down his throat and, as we later discovered, badly scarred his vocal cords. At the same time, the medication also continued to induce weight loss. Chris was in complete agony. He was unable to eat at all due to the pain he was suffering. His only nourishment initially was via straws to bypass the mouth ulcers. All the time he was becoming weaker and gaunter.

On returning home from work early one afternoon, I found Chris had already taken to his bed looking worse than ever. Concerned, I reviewed all the prescribed medication and discovered that while some had known adverse side effects, others should not be taken together. I stopped Chris taking his full prescription and only allowed him the absolute necessary for his diabetes and arranged an emergency doctor's appointment. Chris' immune system had been compromised by the combination of prescribed medication but, although initially confirmed by the health care professionals, nothing was put in writing and eventually he was advised that he'd suffered an allergic reaction to antibiotics to treat his chest infections.

In addition to Chris' health problems, his computer crashed. I was woken during the early hours one morning to find him practically in tears. He had lost over eight months of writing; his entire typescript had been erased. Attempts to retrieve the documents proved fruitless until Chris' publisher intervened; a partial recovery from the hard drive gave Chris some much-needed encouragement. However, important lists and pointers were lost.

This book is more of a journal of the three-year period chronicling Chris' health problems, his treatment, his fears, the support of his friends and the Garden, and his eventual improvement. At the same time it is also interspersed with tales and thoughts of his past. And while this isn't the jovial and light-hearted book that Chris had planned, it is the honest struggle of his recovery, not only from the physical restraints but also from the deep depression his condition caused.

Chris is indeed a most complex person and hopefully this volume will help you know him better, but then, "You can live with someone for 50 years and never truly know them."

Chapter 1

Oh Lord, help me – I want to die

I don't actually want to die but I honestly feel I'm dying.

I'm in so much pain and agony and I don't know how much more I can take.

I lie here resting throughout the day trying to build up enough strength to do my radio show each evening, trying to keep up the pretence that everything is OK. Yet the doctors haven't a clue what's wrong with me. Well, they know the symptoms: I have complete ulceration of the mouth, lips, up into the nasal passages and down the throat. And the weight I have lost is far too great. But they don't know how to put things right. They have all agreed on one thing; it was caused by an allergic reaction to medication. Now, to be perfectly honest, I'm too frightened to take any more drugs in case it causes more harm.

I sit here most days in tears and my only relief is when friends drop by for a short while. But I can sense they are not comfortable: you can see it in their eyes that they wonder if there's more I haven't told them.

With so many bad things which have happened to me in the past, it's difficult to be cheerful at all. I keep hoping that I can 'buck up', but I'm finding it difficult to focus on any good times. I know that if I concentrate on my future, the way I'm feeling now, I won't have one. But if I look to my past, I'm sure I can find those highs to guide me forward.

↕

For a while Gabe and me lived in an old farmhouse just outside Bridgend. It was the place I escaped to. I called the house Southfork, as in the TV show *Dallas*. Next door there was another beautiful house and that actually looked like a ranch! I often saw this lady of exotic appearance coming to and fro. She looked gorgeous and seemed the friendly sort but never got the opportunity to approach her, but I felt I really wanted to. Although it was a wonderful place to live, it could be really lonely stuck out in the sticks, especially as Gabe was out at work during the day and, if he was on visiting duties, he could be anywhere in Wales checking benefits' entitlements and giving advice to vulnerable veterans, and I didn't know if I'd even see him before I left for work in the evening.

It was yet another wet bank holiday and the bin men, as a result, were supposed to be coming on a different day – I'm amazed they come at all. But, I was told that the bin men were actually coming on this particular day. I saw the lady, Pam, dragging her rubbish back indoors. So I, the knight in shining armour, went to her rescue and told her that the bin men were actually on their way. She thanked me and we started chatting. She knew all about me even though she was from Yorkshire, the reason being that her husband Paul was from, guess where – yes, Cwmafan! We hit it off big time. She was so 'gay friendly', loved life and seemed a million per cent more camp than me! God, I'd found a friend who didn't want me for air-time or anything else, other than she just genuinely loved me. I offered her a job as my PA, but she declined it as she'd suffered an accident and was awaiting treatment and didn't feel she'd be able to dedicate the time required. I was gutted. However, Pam would come over to my house and sit at the bar and drink Pimms and we'd put the world to rights!

I'm always on my own during the day as Gabe works 'normal' business hours. When I had my hernia operation it was difficult to even get out of the chair. One particular day, I was sat in the big swivel leather chair, hurting with the stitches etc. and bloody starving, and the next thing Pam turns up with the biggest beef dinner that I've ever seen. It was ecstasy!

We helped each other no end, even went out shopping together – not that I need help shopping, mind. As you know, it's my favourite sport! One day she turned up at my door and said that she and her husband were leaving Wales to go back to live in Yorkshire. I was gutted again. We still keep in touch and I often remind her that when she says to me "anything I can ever do?" that she's in York and I'm in Wales – hardly the situation to drop some shopping in. She recently came to Wales to visit friends and family but I was too ill to see her. I hope we'll meet up again soon, as I miss her; maybe Gabe and me will take the motor home and have a trip up North, and take our dog Buster as well. I wish there were more people like Pam. I think the world of her and Paul.

Diabetes

Don't ever get diabetes for God's sake. It's been the ruination of my life. I thought that when I was diagnosed all I had to do was put a sweetener in my tea. If only!

I've learnt as I've gone along, the hard way. I listen to doctors but it doesn't do anything for me. I need practical help, not jargon. There's one specialist that I just don't get on with at all. For a start, I don't understand a word he says and I couldn't begin to tell you where he comes from. He makes me feel crap and moans like an old fishwife to me. You are obese etc. and you are short-circuiting your life, he says to me. He doesn't realise that he's putting years on me. I've tried to change hospitals but they say no, you can't. Who the hell are they – a bunch of pen-pushers. From now on I will go private. I was put on slimming pills and lost weight in a crazy way and they made me so ill. Never again. God will decide when I go, not some bloody quack with his impossible to understand accent. As far as I'm concerned, when it's my time it's my time – and that's that.

It's so hard watching TV adverts showing cream cakes and TV chefs cooking with sugar and butter; there should be a law against the whole lot. Even when I go to cafés or restaurants there's no diabetic alternative and no sweeteners. Flying is hard work; I don't trust the food on planes. I always order vegetarian options; I never eat meat on planes. When you're diabetic it takes a longer time to heal. If you want something at the chemist they ask you if you're diabetic and usually the answer then is no, you can't have that. How I'd love to sit and have a cake or a bar of chocolate, maybe a packet of crisps or real gravy. It's a load of crap being a diabetic.

If I had my life over again there'd be no sweets or chips. Hard mind you, when your mother had a sweet shop and your father a chip shop!

I wish I had never said a thing...

I spilled the beans about the child abuse I suffered and now wish that I hadn't. Why? Well, now everybody knows and I often get people consoling me, "There, there, it must have been awful." But it went on a lot back then, hopefully times have changed now. I can't forgive people for not listening to me then. People thought I just wanted attention. Shit, I had loads of that. I suppose I was better at handling things when nobody knew but now I have to put up with people coming out with the most stupid things. Most just want to know who my abuser was and they try to work out who it was. Yet they go on to say that it never stopped me from getting on in life. Really? It wasn't something I could bury in the back of my mind. I lived – correction – live daily with the consequences. It makes me laugh sometimes, but a lot of nosey people lived in the village but nobody heard the cries of a small boy back in the 1960s. Strange isn't it? As they say, people only want to see what they want to see.

↕

I've become very friendly with Jamie from Neath – mainly through the entertainment industry. To my surprise I discovered that he's a cancer sufferer and was undergoing chemotherapy and he wasn't at all well during his treatment. I offered to go with him for company. I watched the process: the saline went in first, then the chemo. Jamie doesn't like needles, so I was the obvious choice to lend a hand as I inject myself four to six times a day. I don't think he'd make a good diabetic – needles are a no-go area for him! He seems to be doing OK at the moment; and we've grown incredibly close and often meet up at Georgie's Diner in Pyle for grub. We compare notes on our illnesses and it's quite interesting what gets uncovered. I've got to the stage where I don't give a flying jump. If I feel something, I just say what I feel.

Jamie and me often go to the cooked meat stall at Neath indoor market – it's near the pet stall. The cooked meat has to be the best ever, but the pet stall? Well, I seldom need to go there! Buster hasn't complained yet. But back to the cooked meat. We often have a takeaway beef dinner or loads of roast pork and crackling to make sandwiches with. This does help us a lot, having company and great food. I honestly believe that you can eat your way back to good health. I also think that good entertainment does the same thing. Jamie is the DJ and entertainment manager at Briton Ferry Workmen's Club and that keeps him going. It's the same for me; I often feel dreadful at the beginning of a radio show, but when I open the microphone, look out, I'm taking off baby!

↕

Mouthwash. OK, hardly a low point as such in my life but it's bloody annoying. I've been given a steroid mouthwash and I have to swish it in my mouth for two minutes, four times a day. You can guarantee that someone will call me, knock the door or tap the window right in the middle of it. And if it turns out to be a cold caller on the phone for windows, PPI or energy switchover, well, let's just say they regret having my number!

✚

I'm glad to say that the grand piano is back where it's supposed to be, in the *parlwr* (parlour) at Cwmafan. I once had the grand piano in my flat in Cardiff. It stood in my second bedroom like a beached whale. It had to go. So, one day, when I called my butty, Tim, who has a garage in Laleston, I just happened to mention that I was trying to move a grand piano from Cardiff to Cwmafan. He came up with the solution by putting me in touch with his mate's music shop, and they referred me on to some people who moved musical instruments for a living. I think it was done painlessly for about £100. I was chuffed. It was always something I intended to do but had never gotten round to arrange. I guess, had I never mentioned it in passing when chatting to Tim, it would still be in Cardiff today. The piano was home and I'm sure that that would have pleased my mother no end. I've noticed that old habits die hard; people are once again sat on my front wall listening to me playing just as they did in the old days. This has given me a lot of comfort. A definite high.

✚

Another positive event in my life, although fairly recent, was meeting Ceri Edwards. We were introduced by some mutual friends. She has a hairdressing academy in Rest Bay, Porthcawl. We hit it off pretty quickly and we began to meet up and put the world to rights. She tried straightening my hair – speaking of which – she's been the nearest to actually getting it straight, up to now. As time went on, Ceri and me got to understand each other more and more. It's strange how friendships develop and, after just a few months and a few business transactions, we've become more like a brother and sister. Gabe and me were invited to London to see a show and, as it happened, Ceri was there at the same time. She had tickets for the musical *Legally Blonde*. So after our respected shows, we all met up, including Simon Bowman and a few cast members from *Les Misérables*, and went to Chinatown for an incredible meal. Sometimes Ceri puts on a hairdressing exhibition and I compere the show for her and, all in all, I feel sometimes that we've known each other for ages.

Chapter 2

GABE AND ME love traipsing in the motor home and on one particular trip we went to Calais in France. I wanted to stop at this rather nice campsite just a few miles down the road from the port. We were given a tour of the site which proved to be far superior to the write-up we'd seen, and they showed us where to park the motor home. Included in the charge was use of the electricity box so that we could have electricity just like being at home and, of course, to fully recharge our batteries.

Like being at home, my arse! Now then, at home I have a couple of microwaves and lots of electrical appliances – and the motor home is just the same. I decided to cook an evening meal and used my appliances as I would do so at home. The next thing, all I could hear was all these French do-gooders moaning and groaning as the whole camp went off. I had blown the electricity, as only I can. I never forgot Gabe's words, "You could sit in a Russian tank and bloody knacker it." Anyway, this little French maintenance man was running about for his life, and nobody had any power for cooking or any hot water. Just as well that I had a gas stove on board. I was even thinking of opening up the side of my motor home and selling hot food like a British burger van. Upstairs for thinking, that's me!

I've renamed the motor home – Motor Homo. Well, self evident isn't it! Gabe has a unique car registration, so that has become the Homo Mobile – well, Batman has a Bat Mobile.

↕

One of the biggest highs of my career was meeting legendary broadcaster Beti George.

While I was on Radio Cymru, I was asked to appear on Beti's radio programme called *Beti a'i Phobol*, where people reminisce about their lives, and to make it even more interesting my mother was invited to be on the programme with me.

I gave my mother a lift in my car to the studio, and into the BBC we ventured. I thought she would enjoy a little guided tour but she used the opportunity to put the world to rights and told the writers and actors of Welsh TV soap opera *Pobol y Cwm* what to do etc. I guess she fancied herself as a director! I introduced my mother to Beti and off the programme went. I didn't know what we were going to be asked and I had no idea what my mother was going to say. But, I have to admit that she played the perfect guest and pressed all the right buttons. Beti got on brilliantly with her and often speaks fondly of my mother to this day.

↕

Low points in my life and career are usually centred around prats that want to be noticed, and I no longer suffer fools gladly. I was invited to Benidorm to perform and was asked to travel with some club bookers/entertainment agencies and some venue landlords etc. I was up at the crack of dawn and got to Bristol Airport and said hello to the guys who were waiting to go to Spain. One of the men got a bit drunk – well, fair play, it was 6 a.m. after all – and started calling me the usual queer names. I simply said to the others, "I've had enough. I'm off home. Stuff this." And home I went, on my own, on a bus and then a train. When will these 'men' stop calling me names? I really hate attention seekers. In future I'm going to name and shame them in public. And they call me queer? Personally, I feel that airports shouldn't sell alcohol at all, or aeroplanes and trains either for that matter.

↕

No smoking Britain is definitely a low point – not for me

personally, but indirectly. To me, it all started to go wrong when the smoking ban came in. How do you explain to a working man that he can't go to a workmen's club and have a pint and a fag? Too many do-gooders are trying to make silk purses out of sows' ears.

Not everyone is a toff or well-to-do. There has to be spit and sawdust venues; you have to have a variation to cater for all walks of life. People used to go out to the local club to have a drink, meet friends, see an artiste, have a game of bingo etc. and have a fag! People don't want to stand out in the rain to have a ciggy and be put on display saying, "Hey look at me, I'm treated like a leper." If I wanted to live in East Berlin, I'd have moved years ago. Why do I have to pay so much tax and be told what to do? I don't believe in war, but vast amounts of my earnings go towards funding it from what I gather. I thought I could spend my hard-earned money on what I wanted. Oh, how I'd love to be a politician; all the perks and expenses thrown in. At least that's what it seems. And if I hear one more time of how much smokers cost the NHS – if it wasn't for the taxes on tobacco, the country would be bankrupt and there certainly wouldn't be funding for the NHS at all. I'm not a smoker now, but I feel that their rights should be upheld too.

Early summer 2011

I now feel so ill that I'm half expecting to kick the bucket any time now. I can't walk properly because of circulation problems and, of course, my poxy knee has swollen and is causing more problems when I try to walk. Then I have a throat and mouth full of ulcers which are so bad that I've only been able to eat porridge, jelly and mashed potato for the last three months. I've had every test under the sun which only point to me being run down. Well, if that's the case, I must have been run down by a steam roller! My life has slipped away right in front of me, and I want it to slow down and let me enjoy it for a while.

↕

It's always difficult to think of food when you're not well and can't eat. But, when focusing on the good times and enjoyable experiences, I'm often drawn to Simon's Restaurant in Gibraltar.

Once, while wandering around Gibraltar, living in my own world (planet la-la), pretending that we lived there and carrying a Spanish newspaper to stop Brits bothering me, we discovered the restaurant in Cornwall's Lane. We went in and straight away hit it off with the hostess and waitress, Suzanne, who turned out to be Simon's wife. The food came and my God it was like nothing I'd seen or tasted on earth – absolutely amazing on all three counts: quality, presentation and quantity – this was no nouvelle cuisine establishment. We became great friends with chef Simon and Suzanne over the years and, on one two-week holiday to Gibraltar, I booked me and Gabe in to eat at the restaurant for 13 evenings. Maybe a little obsessive, but that's how much I loved the food and the company. Hell, we had to eat somewhere, so why not somewhere we enjoyed! They hardly ever use beef sirloins in Gibraltar; it's usually fillets and always beautifully butterflied with one of our favourite sauces – so I was away with the fairies. I would even have a drink out there, usually Mateus Rosé wine and, my God, I felt good.

The holiday would come to an end and, once again, I'd start to have the doldrums. I didn't want to go back to Wales. After a few trips we bought an apartment, a second home, so that we always had a bolt hole we could nip to for long weekends. I long for the day when Gabe and me will just go abroad and live there permanently. Unfortunately, Sue and Simon sold the restaurant for an easier life themselves and, while there are many other establishments on the peninsula that offer excellent service and choice, I don't feel any will ever compare fully with Simon's.

↕

Bad hair days – are there any good ones? As well you know, my hair has always been a constant source of embarrassment, annoyance and expenditure. I would literally pay anything – and have done over the years – to have straight hair, and lying here, unwell, makes no difference and has added to the depression I seem to be spiralling into, definitively contributing to my long list on the 'low' column.

I'm sort of managing to straighten my hair with my GHDs, the 'Rolls Royce' of hair tongs, and to be honest it stays straightish unless, of course, it gets wet...

Well, it rains nearly all of the time here in Wales. So, to run to the car I have to put a baseball cap on. Now that will flatten my hair and, after a while, it makes me sweat – so it then curls. If I'm in Spain and I straighten my hair, it's so hot out there that I sweat – and once again, I can watch my hair curl, in front of my eyes even! The dirge of my life!

I've said in my will that when I die I want my ashes to be spread in Spain, and the other request: I want straight hair next time round! I tell you what's difficult – I have to wash the hair and condition it, dry it, then tong it and keep away from rain or steaming kettles at all times, and have a baseball cap to hand at all times. Then, when I bathe the following day, I don't wash the hair again as I like it to give it a couple of days to settle. So then I have to wear a plastic cap in the bath. I have to tong it three times a day and then I have to keep gas tongs in the car and motor home so I can touch the hair up and get rid of the curls. It's a pain in the butt, far too time consuming. God, I wish I had straight hair from birth; it would be much easier, trust me! And before I forget, just to add insult to injury, I have to have three sets of tongs for the three places I live in.

↕

Another of my bugbears, and probably the biggest one at the moment, is that people don't listen.

When I'm out and about, people constantly ask me, "How are you?" I'm sick of hearing it. Often they don't listen to my response and then ask me the same question a few minutes later. It's almost become a greeting, a meaningless phrase. I always try and answer honestly but, of late, I've taken to reply, "Oh, terrible, thank you," to gauge a response. Nothing! Usually I've been ignored and they continue with, "Oh, very good." I have come to the conclusion that people just don't listen or they just hear what they want to hear. I reckon if this country banned the phrase, "How are you?", nobody would speak to each other any more.

I suppose when unwell and feeling so low in spirit I'm no different to anyone else in that I start to think of my family. Unfortunately for me, I stop at my mother and father whom I've lost and greatly miss. It's always been a bit of a hit and miss situation with my brothers. I don't think there's ever been much love there anyway.

I always say "When the mucky stuff really hits the air cooling perambulator," and exactly what happened when my mother died and left everything to me. Now that was big news to me and, whatever I thought at the time, I had to do as my mother wanted. I was too hurt and raw to do anything different to what her will said. Almost immediately, I was dropped like a ton of bricks. Neither of my brothers spoke to me at all after the contents of the will became known. In fact, I don't even know where one of my brothers lives, and there's now another child that I haven't met, but there you go. All I'm guilty of is being a good son.

I've often wondered if we'll ever speak again, but sometimes for me I feel it's too late. I hate sounding bitter, but I'm better off away from the lot of them. At the end of the day it's their loss, not mine – moving on swiftly.

I love my job. I love being behind the microphone and often sit looking at it. I wonder who's going to be listening in tonight, looking for some comfort. The feeling of power is immense as I open the fader and begin to speak. Who's reacting to what I say? Why are they listening, and what are they doing at that very moment?

It's pretty much the same when I'm on stage in a theatre. I look at the audience when I'm doing the funnies and the songs etc. and I can still see the face of my mother in the crowd, smiling her approval. But once off-stage, I can't remember a thing. Did they enjoy? Was it a memorable evening for them? I was in a theatre in the Rhondda a little while back and it turned out to be a very emotional show. There were women crying and hankies in abundance. My last song is always 'I am what I am'. It's the only song that reduces everyone to tears and it makes me feel tingly, as well. I could quite easily cry myself in the middle of the song. And, as a finale, there's no other song that could ever take its place.

↕

Something I really enjoy is making hospital and home visits. This takes some guts to do but, having said that, I've done such visits for years. The thing is that I don't feel like a celebrity and what I have to realise is that the audience think that I am one. To be perfectly honest, I don't do the celebrity bit very well. Mind you, some others at work wallow in it. I can't stand all the bravado. But I do try my best. When I visit somebody at their home, it's usually because the listener is terminally ill and so I have to act accordingly. I don't walk in saying, "There, there." No way, mate. I usually take my accordion and we have a rip-roaring shindig. They are so pleased to see me. "It's the man from the radio," they say and that is special enough. They all seem to have the same carpets and mugs as me and they do what my mother did – they bring out the best china, which is the last thing I want. A mug for me please, every time, love. For me it's important to do these visits, as I find that people and authorities today generally care less and less.

I remember one time when I visited someone in hospital and the lady who'd been quite ill was so excited that she texted about 100 people while I was there just to tell them that I was there. But if it makes them feel good that their favourite radio presenter has called on them, well, so be it. I find that there are a lot of people that have nobody, no friends and no family and that is sad. I try and say the right thing when I visit and I always try to make them laugh because if they do have a chuckle, then you've won. I can actually see the pain of loneliness on their faces, particularly after they've lost their partner. God knows what I'd do if anything happened to Gabe; he's the driving force behind me and he wants me to do what I do, and he loves to help as much as he can. What can I do to bring some comfort to these lonely people? I look at an elderly lady and I think to myself that this could be my mother and then I really turn on the healing process. I let them talk and tell me about their lives. I have to be honest, it's really interesting. If people only took the time to listen and show an interest, things would be a lot different.

I'm so lucky that I have the job that I do. I couldn't see me doing anything else. I want to put the world to rights and I want to take away the pain that people are suffering. Why should people put up with the crap that they do, and it hurts me to hear on the wireless about care homes mistreating old folk. It hurts me that some of these poor buggers don't even get basic things like washing and good food. My God, I'd love to be in power; I'd probably get shot for my boldness. But hey, what can I do except keep on trying, and I will never stop trying to put decent people first. I don't want to know about these louts that cause riots and expect everything for nothing – get a job like me, and pay your own way.

I look forward every time I get a request for a visit. I remember fondly visiting one particular lady here in Wales that had had a mastectomy and, when I went in to see her with a few little gifts, she said to me, "Look what they have done to me, Chris." She said she could talk to me like a sister. But the point I'm trying to make here is, would she have been able to do that if I was a straight man? I wonder. Well, so be it. I just long to do good. I couldn't stand it if I had to tick boxes all day and sign forms. Bugger that. The first thing I usually say to people is, "Now if you want to swear, you carry on." And don't get the best china out for God's sake.

I will never stop doing the visits as long as I live and I know it's not in my job description. But there are two things in life that tell me where to go, and that's my two legs.

Acceptance

Throughout my life I've wanted to fit in, but it's been difficult. People around me, especially in Cwmafan, showed great disapproval and some still do today, especially my family. While growing up in Cwmafan I was called something which a dog wouldn't lick. Gangs of lads would have a field day and my life would sink from heartbreak to wishing I was dead. I once blamed my father, as he was having a right good go at me and I retorted by saying that he should not look at the product, but at the manufacturer. He was not amused by this and exploded again with disgust. Today, it seems it's different for me, but trust me, it's not changed one bit. There are still people that not only laugh with me, but also laugh at me. Some still stand back and don't shake my hand in case they catch something. Believe you me, it's a hard thing to be well known, gay and live in south Wales...

Chapter 3

ON MY GOOD days I can just about crack a smile, but it makes me feel worse when I hear people making up what they don't know. The latest rumour flying about is that I was terminally ill, some sort of cancer. And all because I'd lost so much weight in such a short time. People don't stop to think. I had journalists phoning me up, and business associates asking me if I had something to say – if I ever wanted to talk in confidence then they would always be around for me. I was so upset by this that I told someone where to go: I asked them could I spill the beans, could I whisper in their ear? They agreed and I whispered to them, "None of your damn business. Go sling it." Some people are just concerned about being the first to dish the dirt on someone, anyone. Well, listen to this, I was given tablets that disagreed with me and caused me to have thrush and ulcers in my mouth, neck and throat – and that's it. I wish people would stop shit stirring. Mind you, there's a few I'd like to come back and haunt.

When I'm at my lowest ebb, I can always rely on my listeners, the Garden, to buck me up. The letters and cards I receive are a huge boost to my confidence and esteem, but there are others who are determined to do the opposite. My radio show is by no means compulsory. If you don't like it, change station. I have sufficient listeners – a large following – to justify my broadcasting over the airwaves.

One person, who appears bewildered by my charms, writes:

> Chris Needs. Where did you come from, as you seem as if you
> should not be here with us good people in Wales. You should not

be on national radio as you promote homosexuality. You make it sound as if it's OK to be queer. It is not at all acceptable to be like you and you've convinced the people in your Garden that you are a saint, but you don't fool me, not for one minute. I ask you, as a parent, to do something less public and stop telling the world that it's OK to be like you. If you were my son, I would be destroyed. No wonder your brothers don't speak to you. While I wish you no actual harm, I ask you to consider my words and do the right thing.

My reaction to this is that it sounds to me that you may have a budding gay son or daughter. As I said to my father, take a look at the manufacturer.

↕

Of all the people I've ever met in my life, Mal Pope has to probably be the most talented, trustworthy, genuine and all-round nicest chap that I've come across. The way he lives his life and his belief in the above has helped me carry on with my own life. I've often said that I wish I could be like Mal instead of the mess I've had to endure from the hands of bad people. I was given the part of Joe Gess in his musical, *The Contender*, which was a big thing for me to do as I'm usually a one-man band. The experience was invaluable. Thank you, Mal. We also appeared together on a BBC quiz show, *The Lyric Game*, along with Leo Sayer – another fun experience and, as I was fairly new to the BBC at that time, it was good exposure for me. Mal has produced albums for me and has appeared completely free of charge on my charity shows. When I was on the regional committee for the Variety Club of Great Britain, I was asked to arrange a special event in his honour – the Lifetime Achievement Award. It could only have been the biggest bash ever for our Mally Pops and so, I pulled out all the stops and even had my 'Telly Mam' there, Margaret John. We re-enacted our scene from the show *High Hopes* for Mal. And tributes were made from all sections of broadcasting, sports and musicals. A very personal tribute was sent by Elton John whose company Mal wrote songs for in his early days. It was a very moving event and there were tears galore. Mal is a very popular broadcaster on Radio Wales, a much admired columnist for his regional newspaper and still finds time to write musicals, be engaged in film projects and perform. He is definitely an asset to the whole of Wales, and I'm honoured to have him among my true friends.

↕

Strange how some things just come into your mind for no reason! I had a caller chatting to me on air some time ago, and she just stopped in the middle of our conversation and asked me if I knew what a Shih Tzu was. Naturally I replied, "A dog." "No," she said, "It's a zoo with not many animals!" We both fell about laughing and it still makes me laugh today. A classic, thank you, lady!

↕

A bad night tonight. OK in myself, but just couldn't sleep and couldn't concentrate on the TV or wireless. Again, the memories drift back and I remember two of my dearest friends, Maureen Norton Price (who sadly is no longer with us) and, from Cwmafan, Christine Lawrence. If I was with either of them and we were up late we used to play cards or, was it because we played cards we were always staying up late? We used to play switch and gin rummy. I loved it.

↕

Out of the blue – a lovely letter from Tammy Jones saying how much she enjoys my programme. She told me that she'd been abroad for 15 years in New Zealand and that she was now back for good. She told me that she loved being over there but missed Wales so much. So back she came. We swapped numbers and soon had long chats together. I'm a good judge of people (unless they are mega devious) and I really felt that Tammy was one of the good ones. She was so big back in the

1970s and 1980s, what with her hit record 'Let me try again', and I knew that the Garden people would love to hear her sing again. I played some tracks from her various CDs and told my listeners the story of this lady's return to Wales. They were immediately interested and wanted to know whether she was performing anywhere in Wales. Well, after speaking to Tammy and explaining about my charity fundraisers at the time, she asked if she could be a part of some of my variety shows. I was delighted and grabbed the opportunity with both hands. I asked her about fees and her answer was, "There's no fee as it's for a charity." Now trust me, you don't get that often today and bear in mind that she lives in north Wales and we were talking about performing in south Wales – and we all know what the roads are like don't we!

So, Tammy was on her way to do the show in Swansea's Grand Theatre and I could only remember her from pictures from the old days on television. She'd already explained that she wasn't dark any more but blonde, and that she was excited to meet me too. The big day arrived and we met and what a lovely lady! The best thing for me was that she was true, honest and decent. You could tell a mile off, and this pleased me no end. I watched her rehearse at the Grand Theatre, and she still had it. She performed with the dancers and it was an absolute treat. Well, we hit it off, and I'll never forget her very kind words on the stage at the end of the show and I nearly became tearful. I think Tammy was looking for sincerity and decency too, and we became friends that night.

Since then we've kept in contact and I told her about my previous trips to the north of the Principality and she offered to help set up venues in the region and to appear on my show which, I hasten to add, she has done and has gone beyond the call of duty. What a trouper. She has worked her backside off to help me raise funds and I'll never forget that. It has been an absolute pleasure meeting and working with Tammy. What a good day that was when she wrote to me and sent me her CDs. Tammy, God bless you, cariad.

↕

Pen-pushers get right on my pip and 'pen-pushers' syndrome' is a constant annoyance to me and seems to be evident everywhere these days. For example, I had to phone one particular council office to ask for a final figure for a show that I'd done, so that I could tell the charity how much I'd raised etc. The lady concerned was due to attend a meeting shortly, at 10 a.m., so I asked her to call me back. Nothing that day, so I called her back the following morning and a colleague advised me she was in another meeting. So, I just bluntly told her why didn't she get herself out of the meeting and do some work for a change, which didn't go down well, as if I give a monkeys to be perfectly honest. Could you imagine me saying that on the radio – that we can't have the news at ten as I'm going to a meeting or you can't have an anniversary dedication as I'm not at my desk. Do they have a clue? They need to get their priorities right and if they're unable to complete necessary tasks, then these actions need to be delegated to those who can.

↕

I never get enough sleep, no matter how hard I try. It doesn't matter which property I'm at either. I'm constantly woken by telephone calls, even by those who know I don't get home until after 2 a.m., or there's some meter man ringing the daylights out of my doorbell to read the meter or, if I'm at my apartment, ringing to read somebody else's meter because they're not at home, or cleaners cleaning the communal parts of the flat. This has to be the bane of my life. I can't sleep when I'm supposed to sleep and if I do happen to get off to sleep, nobody will leave me alone. No different if I'm trying to relax and watch TV. This is a physical impossibility. With the way I'm feeling at the moment, if I'm disturbed again by the phone and asked, "How are you?" I will tell them that I've just died! And if it happens to be a cold caller – and they just happen not to withhold their number, they'd better be prepared for calls from me!

↕

One of my dearest friends ever is Christine from Durham. We've probably put a hole in 40 years, me and my Geordie mate. We're still the best of friends and whenever I can find a cheap flight from Rhoose to Newcastle, I'm away. As you get older, you hang on to a true friend – that's if you're lucky enough to have one in the first place. I absolutely love Christine with all my heart and I trust her with my life, and my credit cards! We met way back, when we were in Jersey in the Channel Islands.

She was a holiday company rep and I was entertaining at the Hawaiian Show in St Brelade's Bay. When Christine was on board a coach taking people on a tour of the island, she'd go past my club and stop to tell them all about me, saying that I was the best entertainer on the island and beckon them to the reception to book tickets to see me that week.

Now that's what I call a friend. We went everywhere together; people thought that we were an item, but it never could be. She was the wrong sex for me and I was the wrong sex for her!

I was well accepted by her family back in Durham. Her mam and me were big butties* and I was always welcomed there, Christmas time, or any time in fact! I loved going for a night out with Christine: to the bingo, to the workmen's club and then an Indian supper straight after. I always got her bed – the big double – and she always went in the spare room. But we always ended up in the same bed together, just talking about old times. I'm so glad that I have Christine in my life. She means the world to me.

* If you are not Welsh, a butty is the same as buddy, mate or friend. In this instance, butties is the plural of friend, not chip sandwiches!

↕

Trying to sleep again. I can't sleep at night and I've always been the same. Why, I don't know. There's a number silly reasons, one of which may be that I'm missing something. Does that sound crazy? Well, I'm a crazy bugger! I always have too much to dwell on and I'm always worrying about anything I can get my hands on. I bring a lot of my problems home with me. If someone is in dire straights on my radio programme, I worry for them at home in the night but only because I've been there, clutching at straws myself at times, and I still do, to be honest. I dream and scheme and plan in bed at night, and when it's light I shelve them. But it's good to have a few dreams to fall back on. I've always been a dreamer or, as mother would say, "You're full of it my boy, full of it." Well, she had a point, to be honest.

But I also seem to have regrets in bed at night, wishing that I could go back in time and try again. I hope my twilight years will be happy ones and, more importantly, I want contentment – that would be nice. I've tried sleeping tablets but they make me very thirsty and dopey during the day. What I need is to find a way to try and live my life with a smile on my face instead of concern and worry. It will come right one day for me as long as I have Gabe and my radio show. Here's to a good night's sleep!

Kevin, Dirty Dog

About one minute before I was due to go on stage in Kidwelly recently, I had a phone call on my mobile from Clive, the partner of my friend Kevin.

Clive told me that Kevin had died, which shocked me out of this world. Kevin had lost a lot of weight and was diabetic, like myself. This disturbed me terribly as Kevin was so full of life. As I write this I've yet to tell the Garden, and I reckon some Garden members will be devastated, as the boys were the first gay couple to join the Garden and they were so very supportive of everyone else. I don't know to this day why I haven't popped my clogs. God bless you, Kevin.

↕

Gabe and me went to the funeral and there were loads of people there. To be honest it was as we expected it. Kevin wasn't just well-liked; he was loved with intensity. The chapel was small but beautiful, and the majority of the people who attended had to stand outside in the courtyard. It was the most beautiful service and everyone was so moved with it all. But then came the killer tune: Shirley Bassey singing 'I am what I am'. That was it; I was away and couldn't hold back the tears. There were two gorgeous black horses and a black lacquered coach that took Kev to the place of burial. It was nice to reminisce with everyone back at the Heritage Hotel afterwards but, with my condition, I was unable to eat anything even though the buffet was beautifully presented. I hugged Clive before we left and told him not to be a stranger. I hope he won't be.

The changes to Port Talbot

Now, contrary to what you may think, I used to absolutely love Port Talbot and longed to go there with my friends, especially on the weekends – so many good times and memories. But now I look at Port Talbot with great sadness. To me, the heart has been ripped out of the town with all the changes. The big one has to be the removal of the Beach Hill in favour of a small bypass. I don't think I'll ever get over that. The times my father would take us as a young family down St Paul's Road to my nana's and, when he got to Beach Hill, he would speed up and our stomachs would rise up and down. (You could do things like that in those days; you were allowed to enjoy yourself.) We'd stop at Antolin's for beautiful Italian ice cream – now, sadly gone as well.

Chapter 4

Late Summer 2011

Oh, my God. I genuinely thought that I was going to die. Gabe was beside himself with massive worry and I checked my will and insisted that we got hitched so that Gabe wouldn't have to pay death duties or inheritance tax.

It all began with a mouth ulcer and a bit of a sore throat. Then the sore throat calmed down, but the mouth ulcer stayed. I was given slimming tablets by a diabetes specialist and I was just told to take three a day until whenever! I took them and began to go to the toilet and it seemed as if I was leaking cooking oil. It was dangerous for me to travel too far in case I had an 'accident'. Apparently, I was supposed to take multi-vitamins as well, but wasn't informed of this and gradually I lost more and more weight. But then, after a three-month stint on these poxy tablets, I became extremely ill with repeated sore throats, swollen lymph glands in my neck and dozens of ulcers in my mouth, nasal passages and throat. I couldn't eat, talk or do most things without great effort. I saw several doctors and was given all sorts of advice. One doctor frightened the living daylights out of me and suggested that the reason for this prolonged illness might be because I was HIV positive, as my immune system was obviously damaged. I nearly fell to the floor with fright, as I'd been in contact with lots of needles and had cuts galore, but have never fooled around sexually. I thought to myself, would this doctor have said this if I'd been in his consulting room with my wife and not Gabe? I was bewildered and the weight was falling off me daily and I thought to myself, well, Chris, this is it.

I saw specialists privately and on the NHS. I even tried complementary remedies. In fact, there was nothing I didn't try. The mouth ulcers were so bad that the oral specialist at the University Hospital of Wales took photos and intended to write an article to accompany them for their medical journal. I reckon there must have been about 50 ulcers in my mouth and around my lips. I cried daily and got smaller. I didn't have the strength to dress myself and, one particular week, I'd promised Gabe that I'd look after Buster for him as he had to go away for a week's course. But I was so desperately ill that he had to cancel his course. I was too ill to sleep alone at night and Gabe sat up and watched me as I sort of drifted in and out of slumber. I was really trying to move on and tried to lift my spirits and decided that I should go to my caravan at Trecco Bay in Porthcawl. When I got there I fell on my knees and cried because someone had spray painted 'Queers' on the caravan. I immediately began to worsen and headed back home to Cardiff and told Gabe. I worsened day by day and cried myself to sleep nearly every night. My God, how I began to hate living here in Wales. My early life was enough to put me off, but this was the final straw. The management of Trecco Bay was appalled and came to see me. I was too ill to discuss anything and simply wondered if these bastards would ever be caught. I doubt it. Mind you, if I'd done something wrong, I'd be the first to be caught. I'm sorry if this offends anyone, but I can't wait to move away from Wales. There's been too much hatred shown towards me for me simply being me. People are not like this anywhere else, believe me. What a nasty place this is; you are welcome to it. I wonder if it's just simply jealousy or has someone a vendetta against me. Just too ill to care at the moment and want to move away, badly. I can't go on raising money and visiting people and trying to help people when, in return, I'm called something which a dog wouldn't lick. You are welcome to my share of Wales. It frightens me to be here.

↕

It's five months later now and I'm finally beginning to get better after taking steroids and all sorts. I will never let anyone hurt me again, nor will I take tablets willy-nilly. I'll never trust a doctor again as long as I live and I swear nobody will ever get the chance to have a go at me because I'm gay. I'm gunning for them. I've had to buy new clothes, which is a shame as I had some incredible stuff. Another bugbear is that people are now stopping me on the street and virtually asking me when I'm going to die. There was even a front page newspaper article explaining that I didn't have leukemia and that I'm on the mend now. People love a bit of scandal but sorry, love, there's no scandal here.

My favourite watering holes

In Wales I have three homes: Cardiff, Porthcawl and Cwmafan. Gabe and me have a flat each in Cardiff; then I bought a caravan in Trecco Bay and then, of course, the house in Cwmafan that was left to me after the death of my mother. There have been other properties in between but I suppose we've been downsizing, looking towards our future maybe. I tried renting out a couple of properties, knowing full well that I'd need to redecorate once the tenants moved out. But one house was trashed by people I believed in, people I knew and thought I could trust. Never again. It took me the best part on 20K to put the house right afterwards!

Anyway, I like to eat and I like to eat out and what I eat has to suit me. So now, after a lot of trial and error, I have local eating places off to a tee. In the Cardiff area, I like to eat at the Busy Teapot in Penarth – the food is stunning, out of this world. It's run by two brothers and the food is all freshly home cooked. When I was really bad and I couldn't hardly eat at all, this was the place my dear friend Li Harding took me, and the boys very carefully made a special concoction, under the supervision of Li. It turned out to just simply be scrambled eggs with some grated cheese mixed in. Just remember that I had, and still have some to this day, mouth and throat ulcers. Agony. But between Li and the boys, the Busy Teapot started to put me back on the map. Thank you.

In Porthcawl I've discovered, thanks to the comic Lenny Dee, a place just off the Pyle roundabout called Georgie's Diner. It's open seven days a week from early morning until mid afternoon. It's an old railway carriage that's been done up and extended. I believe it was first of all a driver's truck stop but, if you're expecting a transport caff, it's nothing like one. When you walk in it's like walking into a time warp and it's beautiful inside. Mums, dads and their children, reps and businessmen, drivers – everyone can be found there. It's so well run, no messing, no booking and the food is excellent, all fresh and homemade. They've been awarded a top accolade for food and cleanliness, five stars no less and, just to round it all off, the people that run it are so lovely. Just like the saying goes, 'You could take your mother there.' Try it, and you will be so surprised.

Now we come to Cwmafan. Yes, you've guessed it – the Rolling Mill. It's run by Veronica and Paul, two of the most genuine people that you could ever want to meet. They cook me and Gabe our favourites – fillet steak with peppercorn sauce for Gabe, and Diane sauce for me with onions rings and all the trimmings. The food at the Rolling Mill is second to none; in fact it's the nearest food to my favourite Gibraltarian restaurant, which I've already mentioned, Simon's. All these places have stunning food, great people working there; you can have takeaway dinners and they are all as cheap as chips. Try them sometime and let me know what you thought of them. Bon appétit, flower!

↕

Something that always drags me down is when I've time to take a quick break I just can't get away. You'd think with a major airport on your doorstep it would be easy to do so. Not when it's Cardiff Airport. It's not just that I can't get to the places I'd like to go to, but that the number of flights and destinations are restricted and are decreasing, or at least it appears so. I just don't know why it's so bloody difficult to get flights from Cardiff to anywhere. I have a better chance of flights from Bristol and London. But to me, an airport is an airport. It must be wonderful to live near Gatwick or Heathrow. I do feel sometimes like I live in a Third World country. I just looked a moment ago for a flight to Newcastle to see Christine in Durham, and the cost on my laptop said £60 from Bristol and £298 from Cardiff. God, are we that special here to warrant such a price hike? I don't think so. So why is it so difficult and expensive?

↕

It's not just news headlines or watching TV that annoys me. Just take a look on the streets: any park, bus station, town centre or shopping precinct. Why do youngsters wear hoodies? They look so bloody stupid I think, and probably the rest of civilization think so too. They walk around thinking they are cool but they look so bloody lowlife. I can't work out either why they wear woolly hats in the summer. Then we have the jeans hanging around arses. How the cowing hell do they keep them up? Perhaps a clothes peg attached to their important little appendage? Aren't you fed up of this yob culture and sloppy dressing? It's not as if it's cheap clothing, just cheap appearance. Let the army call the buggers up, I say. Exactly why did National Service conscription cease, I wonder?

↕

I'm not getting on my high horse, but why are so many ideas not carefully thought through – especially without any consultation? It seems that we're now expected to use public transport and leave the car at home. On paper that sounds good, but does it work? Does it hell, my arse! Can you see me travelling home from the BBC in Cardiff by bus to Port Talbot at 2 a.m., and getting a connection up to the village, or travelling from a club or theatre with a PA system.* Hey, even during the daytime, sorry sir – I understand you've done your weekly shopping but I can't allow you on board with more than seven carrier bags! Seven bags? Well, so I'm told. Can this be right? Some people are living in cloud cuckoo-land these days. So, now that we've established that we have to have our own transport, the question is can we afford the petrol? This country is a joke; it would be nice one day to have a jolly band of politicians who cared for us; after all we put them where they are today. Every time I tax my car the price has gone up. I speak to probably more people than most and the norm is, "How am I going to cope? Will I lose my job?" Nothing is easy and I feel so much for the working man trying his best. So, if you see me one night on the back of a bus with all my CDs, ducking and dodging hoodies, you'll know that I'm trying to do my best for the environment.

* Public Address system. You know all the gear, not just a microphone and a set of cables, but an amplifier, two speakers, maybe four, plus their stands etc.

↕

I'd just love to be Prime Minister of the United Kingdom. I would make Wales a tax haven to start with, and all the English, Irish and Scots could travel back and forth buying up duty-free goods and Wales would be a rich Principality. I'd bring back National Service, and all these bloody yobs that like to riot, fight and kick-off in the streets, well I'd send them to do it in Afghanistan, or wherever, and then bring our soldiers back home safe. How dare they create havoc on my streets and I have to pay for the upkeep with taxes and insurance. I'd impose a curfew for troublemakers and evict them from their accommodation. No more freebies; work or starve like I've always had to do. I don't get sick money or holiday money; I'm self-employed and that's bloody hard. Why should these wasters get away with it and, to be honest, I blame a lot of this on parents. I tell you now that no child of mine would be out, at the age of seven, looting. Parents need to take responsibility for their children. This country has turned into a right hole and I'd love the chance to turn the bloody lot around. I would call my political party the PNP party – the Poofters National Party.

Going for gold

I've lost so many friends, all around the same age as me or, more worrying, younger. It's made me think how lucky I am to still be alive. All I seem to say to Gabe lately is that I can't believe that I'm still here, with others who were younger and fitter dying. If you need to be noticed, I reckon all you have to do is lose about seven stone and the nation will probably ask when are you going to die, because that's what happened to me. I've now decided that I'm going to try and have a good time every single day of my life. I have to stop worrying and wondering about things because they're going to happen come what may. I woke up this morning and I said to Gabe, "We have to start enjoying ourselves, because you never know. Old age creeps up on you quickly, so be prepared, my handsome!"

Try a cuppa

I was in Cardiff doing some shopping and banking when I felt a bit hungry, which is never good for a diabetic. So, I popped into one of those leading coffee shop chains in Queen Street and ordered a large tea and a cake. Now, bear in mind one thing, I've got to take insulin before I eat. So, I sipped the tea as I can't drink it hot because of my mouth ulcers, and ate a little cake and then covered the cake with my serviette and nipped into the toilet to inject myself, as it causes the same issues as breast feeding – do you do it in public?

Do I inject myself in public? No, so I go to do it in the toilet. Quite a sensible move, I think.

Now, I was not going to take my tea and cake into the toilet with me, so I leave it covered on the table. When I come back a few minutes later, the staff have taken away my tea and cake which, incidentally, cost me over £6. So I say to the guy behind the counter, "You've taken my tea and cake." I get an "Oh, sorry," and a roll of his eyes. I continued by explaining my need to leave the table, and that the tea was too hot to drink anyway and needed time to cool down. Basically, I was informed that he wasn't allowed to replace the items he'd nicked from my table. All I can say is that the staff who didn't spend all their time talking to colleagues *did* actually clear some tables, but it's a pity they didn't tackle the tables that were overflowing with used crockery and plates. I guess mine was the easy option, being only one setting and a token gesture for all the other customers walking in.

Not so guilty pleasures

What can I say about food? At this present time I'm unable to eat much. I'm losing weight like it's going out of fashion. I can remember once getting up after Gabe had gone to work and preparing myself a cooked breakfast. About eight rashers of bacon, two eggs, baked beans, fried bread, laver bread, mushrooms and a ton of bread and butter and red/brown sauce. Lush! A big favourite of mine was chips and gravy or fish and chips, mushy peas, and curry sauce. I also used to love grilled cheese on a Pyrex plate with tomato sauce and bread and butter. Chili was always a big favourite of mine and Gabe also. Sausage and mash with onion gravy, again to die for. I've always been a mega lover of fish. I used to mix white cooked cod with mashed potato and sprinkle on grated cheese. Cockles, I love loads, and crab sticks. What about a bacon sandwich? Lush – and not forgetting toasted sandwiches. Sunday lunch is wonderful and a Chinese takeaway on the weekend is always acceptable. I have the appetite but not the ability to chew and swallow. How I long to be well again, you have no idea.

Chapter 5

MY DEAR FRIEND Maralyn and I met at the Townsman Club in Swansea in 1972. She used to work in the cigarette kiosk on the stairs on the way in. I'd stop for a chat every night; we got on like a house on fire. She was definitely very Chris Needs friendly, and that was rare. I liked her such a lot, too. I was so proud to be a part of the big city that was Swansea, and I loved rubbing shoulders with the families that invested there, such as the Wignals and the Corneliuses. I felt as if I'd 'made it', playing and singing with Gaynor (aka Bonnie Tyler) and making new friends literally every day. Maralyn was so true to me and, if there was ever trouble with any louts calling me poofy names (Wales is almost full of these), she would go bloody bananas and threaten them big time. I really appreciated Maralyn. I hadn't seen her for many years after leaving the Townsman Club, but I bumped into her at Bonnie Tyler's house one Christmas Day and boy, to me, she was the star of the show. She looked almost exactly as she did all those years ago and I'm glad to say that I'm a good judge of people, because the cigarette kiosk girl ended up as the general manager of the club, later renamed Barons. What a wonderful girl. Maralyn, please never change; stay as you are my flower, love you.

And as for Bonnie Tyler, well, what can I say that I haven't already said on air! A very dear friend who dragged me around the country to play keyboards for her. In spite of her success in music and business ventures generally, she remains a very down-to-earth and homely girl who likes nothing more than entertaining at home.

↕

After work, during this latest illness, I'd come home at about 2 a.m. and struggle into the flat, almost falling over from feeling so weak due to not eating. I'd heat up some mashed potato and struggle my way through a baby plate, which would be half full. I'd then wash my mouth gently with cold water to stop the stinging, and this is what I was like five months into the illness. I'd then climb into bed knowing that I'd not be able to sleep and hoping not to wake up Gabe. A little way into the night, I'd start weeping with depression, as half a year is a long time to suffer from ulcers. Once I started weeping and fretting, everything else came to the surface. I'd cast my mind back to the persecution, the nasty teachers and bullying youngsters. Then I'd start to cry properly. I got very upset at the start of my illness when, as I've mentioned, I discovered that someone had spray painted obscenities on my caravan in Porthcawl. I was devastated when I saw this and it exacerbated my downward slide. I'm reluctant to go to Trecco Bay again, as I want to spend my time with people that celebrate my company and not with people who just barely tolerate me. In the morning, I'd wake and Gabe would be dressing and preparing for work and he'd ask how I felt and I'd say, just the same. He was so worried about me. So worried that he didn't know want to think any more, God love him.

When Gabe leaves for work the loneliness sets in and I begin to feel more ill than ever, but I have to try and get my head together because I have to do my show every night. If I lose that, I'd lose everything. It's just so important to me. I inject myself in the morning and I usually bleed onto my shirt. Then I ask myself, shall I bother changing? Do I really want to go out? Then I remember that I have to get Gabe his paper and get something for tea and take Buster out for a pee. So I have to, and reluctantly dress and wonder who I can speak to. But I have to admit nobody really wants to just spend a while on the phone talking to me as they are so busy or at work. I venture out and get my provisions and I'm bombarded by inquisitive people to check if I'm dying or not. As usual, and like I've said,

I get asked "How are you?" maybe 40 or 50 times, from the bacon counter (which I can't eat) to the petrol station, and out on the street and I never know how to answer, and then, every night, I have to go through the same questions again with each caller on the radio. How are you? How are you? How are you? It's become my pet hate, this question. The real answer is bloody crap, but I can't say that on the radio, or to people in public. I long for the day when I'm asked "How are you?" and I can reply, "Bloody marvellous, thanks!"

↕

I've worked with so many artistes and performers that there's nothing you can't tell me about this business. Show business is the only business that can mix politicians or royalty with the man on the street or in the church. And, in which other business can you really dislike a person but you will still be pleasant to them – on stage only! Since the success of my radio show there've been a certain number of people who'd like to push me under a train or off a cliff, given the chance. They just can't hack it that someone else has done better than them. I know I'm a lucky boy with my work. I sit there playing tunes I love and talking to people that like/love me. I get treated like royalty and recognised wherever I go. I work in theatres while others slog away in clubs; well that's not my fault. I struggled for 25 years carting speakers and keyboards up and down stairs, and in and out of estate cars. You get out what you put in, and when this chance of a radio show came along, I went for the jugular, otherwise there would be someone else sitting in my chair.

I worked with a girl fairly recently who said that she thought I loved myself so much that she thought that I'd like to make love to myself. She said that people like me got on her nerves while she had to sing her brains out for a pittance. Sorry, but not my problem. If she was a nicer girl, she might get a hand up the ladder but, alas, she won't get any help from me. I love to see people get on, but people like her should realise that those you upset on your way up the ladder, you end up meeting on the way down again. But then, how many rungs will she climb up with her attitude anyway?

↕

No man's time. This is what I call the time when I'm waiting for the painkillers to kick-in. The pain is making me more irritable today and that has not been helped by the number of cold callers I've had on the phone. I'm convinced that each call centre receives the same sheets of numbers to annoy people and, today, my name and number has cropped up on them all. Although I have a call display, you can't 'police' every contact. When I get a suspect number come up, I've taken to answer, "Hello, South Glamorgan Morgue," and then the phone goes down, and eventually my number gets taken off their system.

And I still get calls for Mrs Needs and I politely ask when did they speak to her last and the answer is usually, a few weeks ago. So then I say, "Well my love, you must have dug her up then!"

Chapter 6

The Muriel (my favourite malapropism)

Have you ever been featured on a mural? Well, a first for me. I was booked to perform at Blanco's Hotel in Port Talbot and saw a huge mural featuring all local famous Welsh personalities in the foyer. I spent a few moments placing names to the faces and then focused on one that seemed more familiar than the rest – it was me! I'd heard mention of it in the past, but had completely forgotten about it. On coming face to face with myself, as it were, I couldn't have felt more pleased, and to be officially recognised in my own country too. I tell you, it's going to be hellishly difficult to remove me from this wall without ruining the whole picture. I am here to stay, baby!

On the bill at Blanco's Hotel was Dame Mandy Starr, the opera diva from Ebbw Vale, and then, of course, me. We got there and were given a really nice bedroom to change in, which was quite close to the stage. It was on the first floor but they had a lift, thank goodness, as I was still weak and had problems with climbing too many steps. It was a dinner and cabaret evening, which was a nice change, and me and Mandy started to get into the mood for a rip-roaring show. While I was by the bar (I seldom drink these days, so I was only getting some sparkling water), this lovely girl started chatting to me as if she'd known me for years and, for a few moments, I couldn't quite place who she was. Then it dawned on me. It was Angie, who was part of the family that owned Taff's Bar in Benidorm. I immediately began to feel homesick for Benidorm and didn't feel I wanted to go on stage that night, well, not in bad weather

Wales when there was beautiful weather Benidorm just a short flight away. I questioned her to see if she missed Benidorm, and did she like it here? Yes, she liked it here, which wasn't what I wanted to hear. Well, what will be, will be.

Anyway, Mandy went on stage and, as large as life, started her set of songs. I noticed there was a table right in the front that talked for Wales; in fact they talked for the Northern Hemisphere. My God, Mandy was singing the longest and loudest note there was from *Phantom of the Opera* and I could still hear this girl telling her friends where she got her bracelet. I have to be honest, I've never heard such a loud table in decades, and people were giving them looks that would kill. I just couldn't believe how rude they were. All of a sudden Mandy stopped the show and turned to the noisy table and said, "Would you like my microphone just in case the rest of Port Talbot can't hear you?" And, to be honest, I don't think it registered with them. They were so wrapped up in their own noisy little world that they were oblivious to everything else. The audience applauded Mandy and the show went on, but so did the noisy table. Well, eventually, some people had had enough and they did their own thing – the noisy women left the table, but their boyfriends didn't. The lads were quite well behaved (sorry girls) and, I have to be honest, if my wife was causing a disturbance I'd have to tell her to wrap up – but that never happened – other people had to do it. I received several emails about the incident and you could tell that there were Port Talbot people there that night who had purely come to see me, which pleased me no end. As I've said, I've always found it hard to be the celebrity in my own back yard. The rest of the audience loved the show and made me feel different about Port Talbot. They do like me, I thought.

The end of the show came and I was glad to be honest, as I didn't have the strength to fight the world and their friends. But, as I got in my car, I discovered that I'd lost my credit cards. I was panic-stricken; I had the management searching the hotel and Mandy searching my car and, eventually, I found them.

They'd somehow got into my music case instead of my man bag. Panic over, thank God, but your heart sort of misses a few beats when panic sets in, and I felt so sick. Afterwards, I just felt so relieved and grateful. And, on the way out, I was asked to sign the mural and was very proud to do so. I felt at long last that my home town was proud of me and there I was, in the Hall of Fame, alongside Michael Sheen, Anthony Hopkins and Rebecca Evans and loads of others. Thank you Blanco's Hotel. PS: the food was incredible – try it sometime.

$$\updownarrow$$

I absolutely love old telly programmes for a couple of reasons – the acting was good and times were wonderful. I love the old black and white movies, especially the old war films like *Carve Her Name with Pride* and *A Town like Alice*. I remember once, one of the newspapers was giving away a DVD every day of classic old films. By the end of the giveaway I'd amassed loads of the old war films. Well, I think I must've locked myself away for about two months. It was heaven. Quite often I close the curtains if I'm at my mother's house and I then feel as if I'm back in the 1960s or 1970s. I once paused a film and started to make my mother's tea! Talk about living in the past – at that point she'd been dead for ten years. I seem to only 'live' in the past, as today I'm merely passing through, en route to the good times. Wouldn't it be lovely if we could just switch the clock back; they were better times then. One of my favourite films has to be *The Red Balloon* which was set in Paris, France, and it's about a young lad and a red balloon which befriends him and follows him around everywhere. At the end others get to see this wonderful friendship and they set out to destroy it. This film has won numerous awards, including an Oscar for best writing – the only short film ever to have had that success. I also love the *Carry On* films and *An Audience with Kenneth Williams*. I adored the comic genius of Morecambe and Wise and loved that scene when Shirley Bassey wore a boot walking down the steps on their show – a true classic. Not forgetting also the episode of *Blue Peter*, with Val Singleton and the baby elephant pooing everywhere!

I look at the satellite TV guide these days and there so many TV stations and I'm still lucky if I find one or two programmes that I want to watch. There are so many repeats, whether it's an hour later, a day later or simply repeated constantly throughout the following weeks. Have we got it right today? I'll leave you answer that one.

A moment of hurt and the 'Cone of Shame'

As I'm writing, I'm looking at Gabe's dog, Buster Llŷr. He cut himself on a sharp branch while out and about, and the wound wouldn't heal. We packed him off to the vets and he's returned having to wear that sort of lamp shade to stop him scratching his neck, as he's picking the cut open all of the time. The vet told us it was completely necessary. Buster keeps looking up at me as if he's about to burst into tears and all I can do is talk to him with as much love as possible and try and make him feel as if I approve of the damn thing around his neck. It's a cruel world, is it not?

$$\updownarrow$$

Gabe and me used to go to a pub restaurant, the Bear Inn in Llantrisant, and we became quite friendly with the landlord and landlady. One day I turned up at the Bear Inn with a CD and on it was a song called 'Oi Mush' with a little more than a bit of 'choice language' on it. We played it privately for our friends, and a few select others were invited to hear it as they thought it was so funny. In fact, it was so well received that a couple of younger lads pinched the disc. I'll never forget the landlady tearing out to the chip shop opposite and apprehending these lads. I thought she was going to explode, and in Welsh to boot! We got the CD back but I understand the lads were banned from the pub for a while. Silly boys, really, if they'd only asked, I'd have got them a copy – after all I am a DJ, so they say.

‡

I've known Marie St John, the Port Talbot songstress, since I was a teenager. I met her at concerts and played keyboards for her. We became great friends; you know when you've clicked with someone and, by damn, we clicked big time. I used to have issues many years ago of being called names by my wonderful Welsh compatriots, but Marie's door would be open for me 24/7, even when she was entertaining or had company. She would welcome me into her house and talk me around from all the name calling. I got to know her dad really well – Ivor or 'Ivor the Engine' as I always called him. Ivor loved my dirty jokes, well, not actually dirty, I like to think of them as 'shop-soiled', and we became good friends.

Now, back in January 1982, the snow came down like the South Pole, and they were cut off where they lived and I came to the rescue. I nipped over to my mother's shop and walked from Cwmafan to Penycae in Port Talbot through the snow with my little box of groceries. I was knackered by the time I got there but, yet again, was welcomed like royalty. While I was there in Marie's house, I was asked to take a look up in the loft to see if there was a leak, being as I was very small in those days (and, to be honest, now as well). I slipped up through the little trapdoor in the ceiling and, to my surprise, I discovered that snow had got in through a hole in the roof. So I cleared the snow and mended the hole with whatever I found up there in the loft and came back down. Boy, oh boy, I was in their good books – mind you, I always was. Marie's dad was quite unwell and I had this knack of cheering folk up, so that was my thing to do when I visited. Marie used to have French students to stay from time to time, some of which are still in touch with her and have even named their French children with Welsh names. Mind you, there was one student from Paris who was a right horrible cow. I didn't like her and she lacked respect. I remember asking her to come to one of my concerts but she was a little unsure if she'd like it. So I tried to coax her by saying "Oh, you must come." But she took that as being literal and said to me "I must come?" as if it was an order. So in the end I told her very impolitely to naff off back to Paris.

I really liked Ivor the Engine and I could see that his health was worsening. I remember the day he died. It was a Christmas morning and I was booked to perform at a club and, as I drove past, I saw Marie sat on her doorstep crying. Her dad had died in the armchair in the lounge. I consoled her but couldn't stay long. I had to go – the show had to go on, and all that show business tradition. I felt so heartless but had to leave her, promising to return later as soon as I'd finished. I didn't think her Christmases would ever be the same again.

But on a happier note, when he was well, Ivor was such a character; you couldn't help but to like him and we got on famously. I remember me and him were on our way to see Marie for a special lunch. I'd picked him up as promised, but we stopped off for a few rums en route and when we eventually got to Marie's, late as hell by the way, the dinner was spoilt. Marie was on the warpath, but we always look back and laugh. I'm trying always to get Marie to sing at one of my concerts. Perhaps one day, if I nag enough!

Chapter 7

Christmas week, 2011

Well, what a year it's been. I'm glad to see the back of it. I'm sat here watching *Celebrity Mastermind* and I've hardly the strength to press the buttons on the remote control. I've been ill since April of this year, not being able to eat or swallow food, losing nearly seven stone. I've discovered that when I stopped taking certain tablets that were given to me by a specialist, I began to get better. My God, you put your life in their hands, but I'll never do that again. The tablets have caused massive problems for me and now I find that I can't sing any more and can barely talk. I'm so hurt and destroyed by all of this, as I'm only guilty of trusting a doctor. My arms measure two-and-three-quarter inches in diameter across and I really look like I've been starved in a concentration camp. I'm stopped everywhere I go, and people ask me how I am and I don't know what to say any more.

I'm not supposed to talk in the day, at the moment. They call it 'voice rest' but, wherever I go, I get asked 20 questions. I tell them, in a low voice, that I'm not supposed to talk in the day and that I need to save my voice for the evening otherwise I wouldn't be able to continue in work. And then, people quiz me more and more. My God, how careless can people be? I'm filled with hatred because of what's happened to me. I can't eat certain foods, but I still have to cook things for Gabe that I can't eat. Then I have to work with singers, knowing that I can't sing anymore. What have I done to deserve this? What harm have I done to anyone? I've cancelled nearly all of my outside bookings which has nearly destroyed me. It's the attitude that gets me. My GP said the other day, "Oh, we'll get you sorted out in a couple of weeks." So I reminded him rather sharply that this has been going on for nine months and that I've been to Harley Street several times and I'm still ill, so what the hell was he going to do?

↕

I've just heard that Maria, who used to work in the shop in Cwmafan, died on Boxing Day morning, at the age of 51. I'm gutted. I only saw her a day or so earlier. As I was walking up the street we stopped for a chat and she laughed so much because Buster was dragging me up the road. Then, a day or so later, she died. Unbelievable. If I'd died people would have said, "Well, he'd been ill for some time." This New Year has to be an improvement. I have to try and stop churning myself inside out about dickheads.

↕

I've now developed a cough and it's hurting me in my chest when I have a coughing fit. My God, I need to sit on a hot beach. I'm gonna have to move to somewhere decent. I'm so weak after those damn tablets I was given. I will never forgive that doctor. He should have tested them on me first. No trial period, no review, no instructions and, it appears, no recourse either. My vocal cords are so badly damaged with scarring that I've been advised it's unlikely that they will ever fully heal. I feel evil, as I can't sing any more. My livelihood. What am I to do? I can't imagine not being able to walk on a stage to entertain. That's my job for God's sake, and someone has taken it away from me. Am I getting better? I'm not sure. No two days are the same.

↕

It's been so damned hard to write this book. I started, then became very ill, but struggled through, writing night after night after work to try and keep my mind off being ill and then, all of my work on the other computer disappeared. I remember going into Gabe's bedroom in the early hours, waking him in a panic, telling him that everything had been deleted. Some friends I know tried to retrieve it, but to no avail. Fortunately my publisher asked for the computer and he found someone who could do the job. At least I got some of it back. But I must admit I lost all my enthusiasm for quite a while before I could continue.

↕

What would I do without Janice Long? I finish work at about 1.20 a.m. and head home to wherever we are staying at that particular time. The radio goes on for Jan's show, keeping me company on my journey. I guess others feel the same about me and my programme. I adore her and I was gutted when her programme was shortened by an hour. She told me that she tried to phone me on my show one night for a chat on air, but couldn't get through because the lines were so busy – the story of my life.

She said on air, on her programme, that she knew I was ill and wished me well. What a legend! When she was working in Cardiff once, she popped into my studio to see me. Boy was I made up. I'd love to work at the London studios and drop by to surprise her!

Memories growing up in the village

I was brought up in Cwmafan, near Port Talbot, and my first home was in Copper Row, a little one-up, one-down miner's house and, if you were posh, you had a lean-to out the back where the coal was kept. They were typical terraced cottages in which you stepped out of the front door and straight onto the pavement. Our front gardens were across the road – I always thought that that was weird. Anyway, our house, number 20, was different to the rest as it was the one with two steps jutting out onto the pavement; everyone else walked straight from the pavement into the hallway. I remember oilcloth on the floor, very high beds, being bloody freezing and having about six blankets over me during the night. My father was working in the dry dock at Port Talbot and he then moved jobs to be a mechanical foreman at the steelworks, which is when my parents then bought the house that I have today in Cwmafan. My mother wanted big things in life and this was just the start, a big four-bedroomed house with a garage and a pit. My father's health was getting worse and he left the steelworks and that's when mother stepped in with the shop. By then, we had a Hillman Minx car, which she liked, but she always wanted a Mercedes. There weren't too many cars on the roads in Cwmafan then, just some buses. And there was the occasional horse and cart back and forth too, mainly the rag and bone man. But I loved it when Mr Morris, the Betterware man, came to call, as he had a suitcase full of merchandise and he always gave free samples to me. I used to hide the free samples, as nothing was sacred in our house.

I liked Cwmafan School and my teacher, Mrs Bailey. We are still friends as I write. She nurtured me in music and I loved it. That was my first delve into music – I owe it all to her.

As the roads were quiet back then you could cross quite easily. Unlike today when it's like Brands Hatch and you risk your life trying to cross. You really have to make a dash for it as they drive far too fast through the village. The pace then was nice and, on Sundays, my mother and father would take me up to the mountain above Cwmafan, to the Seven Winds where all the roads had farmers' gates, and I had to get out of the car and open them all for my father to drive through. He used to tease me and pretend to drive off. He always stopped, but it did worry me being left up the mountain on my own, just in case that pig of a man was around (the one who abused me). I always felt safe in the car or in the house, but never outside. People frightened me and I was right to fear some of them, too.

I was always glad that our house had those steps outside the front door – that made me feel safer.

I never mixed much as I was too frightened to do so. So I threw myself into music, and the piano was my saviour. I used to go to a piano teacher from the age of five, to a Miss Williams who lived twelve doors away, and I took to it like a fish to water. My bedroom was quite a size, as I had the pick of the house (an only child back then!) and I had a piano upstairs and downstairs, and speakers and gramophones. My mother would call my bedroom Jodrell Bank.

When we moved into the house it had gas lights and red flock wallpaper, just like the Indian restaurants at that time, and high fireplaces. Coal fires, an outside toilet, and a bosh with one tap, all cold of course. My Uncle Mal used to joke about the tiles on the roof, as there were a few missing. He reckoned that they blew off due to unexpected wind. My Uncle Mal was a scream and always had a good line or joke to spin. While driving he would toot his car horn to a smart woman walking up the road and say to me "That's my ninth wife" and then he'd see someone else and say that she was his eleventh wife and I used to believe him! His wife, my Auntie Hilary, was so lovely. She was my father's sister and I always had an incredible welcome when I called there. She used to work in an ice cream shop and boy, was I spoiled. The only schoolboy with three flakes in my ice cream cone!

I had some nice aunties in those days. My Auntie Betty, another of my father's sisters, worked on the buses as a conductress and she always gave me the world. Needless to say, I travelled the lengths of the land. Sadly she died a few years ago but she'll never be forgotten by me. My other auntie was Ann, who lived at Porth in the Rhondda. She was a district nurse and delivered babies and tended people galore. We generally went to Porth on a Sunday in our new Vauxhall Velox, and we'd have tea with Auntie Ann and Uncle Alf. It certainly was 'eat up, you're at your auntie's' time. Perhaps it was a throwback to the war years when they had nothing.

These days food is plentiful and readily available and we shouldn't be denying ourselves.

Coming back over the Bwlch towards Cwmafan, we always listened to *Sing Something Simple* with the Cliff Adams Singers on the wireless, and I loved it. My father whistled all the way home. He had the most aggravating whistle I'd ever heard and I used to hold my ears. I had some friends in Cwmafan, but not a lot as I didn't like football, fighting or girls, so I didn't have a lot in common with them. My love was music and that was that. I didn't want to be like the people around me and I guess I'm still like that today. I remember my teacher asking me what I wanted to be when I was a big boy. Others would say a solicitor or a racing driver, but I'd say "a star, Miss" (and I'm still waiting). All I ever wanted was to be on the stage, TV and radio. Mind you, my mother pushed me and my teacher, Mrs Bailey, did as well. At school in Cwmafan I was in everything performance-wise, from reciting, dancing, playing the piano, singing and anything I could get my mitts on. I was always ill on sports day and that was that. I used to watch Welsh TV a lot, adoring Ryan Davies and Iris Williams and all the great Welshies. I'd study Ryan and I learnt a lot from him. My mother was his biggest fan and her front room was like a shrine to him. I remember introducing Ryan's daughter, Bethan, to my mother in Cwmafan and when she sat on the settee my mother starting crying. She couldn't believe that Ryan's daughter was sat on her settee. She swore that she'd never wash the cushions ever again.

↕

I'm sat here typing away and wonder when will I ever be able to eat properly again. Ten months into the illness now and still losing weight, albeit more slowly, thankfully. I can still only eat mashed potato, porridge, jelly, rice and baked beans. Will I ever be well again? I'm beginning to wonder. What will be my future? I could cry to be honest, as all I did was listen to a doctor, but no more. I'm going to be so vigilant from now on. I'm helping Gabe in the shop at the moment and it's spooky as I keep expecting to see my mother popping in.

Not a lot has changed in Cwmafan to be honest. It looks much the same now as it did in the 1970s. I used to go out to play with my gambo, a homemade go-cart, which I loved. I fantasised that it was a posh car and that I was driving it to Swansea. When that became a reality I couldn't believe it. There was a cinema in Cwmafan called Ebley's and I liked going there to see films from all over the world.

I used to fantasise about having money, a boat, a posh house, being famous, but never wanted the Bond girl... no way, just Bond!

We had lovely outings when I was young, as we always had a car. My mother saw to that. One memorable trip was to Pontypridd market and that's where I got my tortoise, Jimmy. There was always somewhere to go and, thanks to the car, we went to places that others couldn't, as they were stuck with going on the bus. Once we went to Penclawdd to pick cockles. That was so much fun but my back didn't think so – bloody agony. The car rides were always a surprise. The destination depended on my mother's mood that day.

She used to jump in the car on a Friday night and drive to Pyle to listen to my radio show on Touch AM as the signal just about reached that area, and she would sit there and listen to every word I said. What a critic – the best. She loved to be included somewhere or other, and taught me never to slag off anyone's family, just your own. So I put that into practice.

Once I said that my mother had a leading part in a Steven Spielberg film, hardly any acting involved and the film was called 'The Mother from Hell'. She loved that and I had to think up things like that all of the time, just to include her and keep my cap straight. People would say to her in chapel or bingo that they'd seen me on TV and she's reply something like, "I can't keep up with him, he's so busy in show business." She loved the fuss and the attention, and who wouldn't.

People would ask how many children she had and she'd reply "Three, one of each." Forever the comedienne! One of the highlights was when she was asked to appear on *Wedi 7*, the S4C programme, one Christmas. I remember once introducing my mother to Dot Squires. Who was the star? It was hard to tell.

Me and animals

In the past, I've always said that my favourite animal is on a plate – until now. Gabe brought Buster home and I freaked out telling him to get rid of him and that I'd give him £2,000 to do so. No way would Gabe get shot of him then and today I'm so glad. I've never had a dog and Buster and me are now the best of friends in the world. In fact, I'd crumble without him. I've never seen such love in my life.

I'm so much for animals now, it's crazy. I love meeting other pets and I adore taking Buster for a walk, or should I say him taking me for a drag. I've never seen such a strong dog in my life.

He knows that I'm ill and he cries in front of me if I start coughing or whatever. I have to admit, at times, I feel as if my time here on earth is very limited. After what I've been through I'm surprised that I'm still alive.

Chapter 8

New Year 2012

I'm praying that 2012 will be kind to me. I never want to even speak about 2011 ever again.

I still want to see the world. So I'm determined to get through my illness and get my life back.

It's New Year's Eve, 2011, and it's a Saturday. I never do a radio show live on a weekend, but tonight is different. For a start, I didn't think that I'd be alive and I always remember my mother's words, "Christmas and New Year are dangerous times for some people; watch out for them and help them." So I'm on air tonight and so is poor old Gabe. God, he's knackered as he's running the shop single-handed because he lost the girl who was going to do half a week for him. Someone said to me today, "Don't wash your clothes on New Year's Day; you'll wash your luck away." I answered, "I hope so because the only luck I had last year was bad luck!" What will tonight bring? Maybe I'll let you know later, that's if I'm not busy washing clothes.

↕

I'm listening to the radio while covering for Gabe, so that he can have a break. They're playing hits from the 1980s and the songs are taking me back to all the good times. And it's got me thinking how lucky I am to be alive right now after what I've been through. If it wasn't for Gabe taking the tablets away from me – he had a feeling it was those damn pills, and he was right. Without Gabe reviewing all my medication I'd be dead by now. I've got some very big decisions to make soon if I want to continue living with a smile on my face.

I used to worry about what I said and what people said, but not any more. Hardly anybody cares – people only care about themselves these days. My life has been in limbo over the past year and that has changed me, big time. I don't need to be liked and popular; I just want to live my life with a grin on my face.

There aren't enough hours in a day. It seems to be work, bed, work, bed, nonstop and nothing else. Oh, I'm dying for a long spell in Spain in the sun. I know it's winter time and the skies are supposed to be grey, but the weather is getting me down big time in this country.

My friend Carole Rees Jones has a beautiful villa in Spain, a pool, the lot, and she tells me to go out there and stay whenever I want. The trouble is I might not come back. I don't want a week in the sunshine, I want a lifetime there – a one-way ticket and a box of matches to burn my bridges with. One day flower, one day.

Being in the shop helps Gabe and gives him some time to see his mam, although usually it's time to keep the accounts up-to-date or deal with suppliers or even nipping off to the Cash & Carry for a top-up. It's been really difficult to find staff. We've both tried so hard to get someone to cover in the shop, even for a few hours, but it seems nobody wants to work – financial downturn, my arse. It makes me laugh.

It may sound strange but I've enjoyed my trips to London. I know that I've been visiting the capital for private medical treatment but it's given me the opportunity to get to know it a bit better. Before, I only knew where the airports were and, of course, the Palace. I'm not fussed about the train service; in my experience they are cold, expensive and late and I end up rushing to get to appointments on time even though I've allocated more than enough time for the journey. I like the taxi drivers in London though; they are real stars.

As I've said, I'm longing to work in London. I'm totally smitten by the place. I walk around Oxford Street performing my favourite sport, shopping! On my last trip to London, I sent a text to all my friends which read, "I'm off to see a top specialist in Harley Street, London; please say a prayer for me that Zara has my trouser size in stock!" The only advantage of travelling by train I can find, at the moment, is that I can book a seat in a quiet compartment. This means I'm not going to be disturbed by other people's loud conversations or that I'm going to be spoken to. I'm supposed to be resting my voice as much as possible during the day to ensure that the healing process continues. It also means that I'll be able to cope with broadcasting in the evenings. I'm not sure what I'd do if I couldn't continue working. What would I have left? At the moment my speech on any given day is very limited and the scarring to my vocal cords is so severe that it's unknown whether or not I'll be able to sing again – talking itself is a painful enough task. How can I face never being able to walk on a stage and entertain? I'd rather die.

On top of all the health problems I have, I've had yet another bad cough for about six weeks and it's nearly put paid to me. It's been like a whooping cough and the weather has been real minging. I'm just wondering who the hell passed this on to me.

It's so hard to keep going when you're not well. I seem to dwell too much on my past and the bad fortune I've suffered. I'm seriously considering counselling for the child abuse I went through but I'm not sure if it will do any good after all this time. It's killing me inside when I think it may not have happened just to me. It's doing my head in. What a way to start the New Year.

It's good to have dreams and goals. Mine is to get a call to cover a show on BBC Radio 2. Just imagine waking up every day in London. Wow. Nobody calling me 'butt' – that would be a good start.

I'm annoyed with myself that I was too ill to go and see Owen Money's pantomime last year. My coughing would have closed the show down! I love seeing Owen on stage doing his comedy act – he shines there. I've been on the blower a lot to Roy Noble lately; we always put the world to rights. I said to him, I remember donkey's years ago, seeing a man walking around with a clapperboard saying "The end of the world is nigh" – and to think, I laughed at him! How bloody right he was; just look at the state of the world today. It's hanging by a thread.

I'm absolutely dying to go to Benidorm but I'm worried in case I have a bit of a turn out there – still can't eat properly. I think we'll have to take the motor home out somewhere for the day soon. That'll be a run for Buster Llŷr as well, and he can enjoy himself somewhere new also.

I'm sat in Gabe's new sweetie shop trying to work out the running order for my birthday show at Swansea's Grand Theatre. This one's going to be the best yet! A real spectacular!

I like the idea that people with not a lot of money can afford this show. I keep the ticket prices to a minimum and the artistes just give me their time – that's priceless. I used to think, who the hell knows me? An old queer on the Welsh radio. But they do, and the big stars want to be on my show. It must be popular. I'm quite often telling the world that I'm gay because I can. I'm fed up with hiding and being questioned. Like I say often, "I'm not perfect but I'm gay and that's close enough."

Omelettes tonight as there's lots of eggs left over in the shop. Just like the days of my mother when we'd ask "What's for tea mam?" and she'd say "Two packets of ham; the date's up today." And that's how we lived years ago – off the waste!

I'm thrilled at the moment because I'm seeing the godchildren. Sam's mine and Sophie is Gabe's goddaughter. They are wonderful children. They are always happy and contented and enjoy coming over to the shop to see us. It's nice to be loved just as you are – brilliant. When Sam finishes a conversation on the phone with me he always says "love you" – no prompting, and that's something you just can't buy.

I've met some interesting people by being in the shop, new folk in the village from a different generation to me. But at the moment I'm really fed up of seeing people struggle just to pay their bills and buy food. It's a sorry state.

Travel – never far from my mind

I remember looking at our old black and white Ferranti TV set, with two big knobs at the front. Years ago they used to show public information films and travelogues. In particular, I recall films about Austria and Switzerland and, from that moment, I fell in love with foreign parts and Wales seemed less interesting. I knew enough about home, but wanted to live somewhere else.

I loved living in Holland. My God, that was one liberal place. I remember speaking to my mate's mother, who must have been in her seventies. She was a Dutch lady and would say that she had to go and watch her favourite programme on TV as the star of the show was a flicker (a gay) and she'd say that Holland was proud of him as they loved flickers. I wished that Wales were like that. I adored Dutch food, especially *boerenkool*, which was mash with Dutch cabbage/kale, served with Dutch sausage.

There was also red pork in Holland which was incredible. But their best food was fries with mayonnaise. I loved Holland as they accepted me. In fact, it felt as if it was almost compulsory to be gay out there. Pity it wasn't like that where I came from; all I got was ridicule every day of my life. It's strange now, as those people who took the mick out of me are now my fans. Work that one out!

Now the big one was Spain. I never felt that I had a home until I discovered Spain. I stepped onto Spanish soil and I felt as if I'd arrived. I didn't want to go back to Wales ever again. In fact I stayed there for 20 years and the only reason I came back was because my father was ill and, while I was here, the BBC opportunity happened and then I stayed for my mother after my father died. I've always found it hard to settle here, putting up with the gay names. I used to answer to some names they called me – I was getting used to it. But, I longed to go back, but couldn't leave my mother as she was destroyed after the death of my father. Mind you, looking back, I should've stayed abroad and brought my mother out there with me for a few months at a time. When she did come out on one of her rare jaunts, she'd speak Welsh to me and then I'd be there speaking Spanish to everyone else.

My intention now is to sell everything and just go back to Spain and that's that. I've told Gabe that if I die here in Wales, he must cremate me and scatter my ashes in Spain.

Lost Opportunities

Back in early spring 2011, I was preparing to play the part of Dylan Thomas in Swansea. It was a reading of the transcript of an original radio broadcast of the famous Kardomah Boys from Swansea over six decades previous, and in front of an audience. The hard part was getting Dylan's mannerisms and speech pattern right. So, I sat down with Swansea producer, Binda Singh, to study this part which was completely new to me. After all, this man, Dylan Thomas, was a big name in Wales and I thought I'd better give it my best shot. Binda was so pleased with what I'd done and his co-producer, Karen Struel-White was on board too and really helping me. It was all going well until my condition worsened significantly. The sore throat got worse and worse and people around me began to wonder what the hell was wrong with me. I felt worse every day and the ulcers in my mouth and my throat meant that I couldn't swallow or eat. I became more upset by the hour. Needless to say, the Dylan Thomas episode went out of the window.

I became worse still and Gabe had to drive me to work and then take time off work himself to look after me. I began to lose work on the radio and I can remember the sleepless nights in Gabe's room – me propped up by pillows in case I choked and

Gabe sat in a chair all night, checking on me in case something happened. Over the next eight weeks I lost seven stone in weight. I never got to play Dylan but, you never know, it might happen again. Binda is very pro Chris Needs. Knowing him, he'd make it happen now that I'm on the mend.

Talking of which, I was leaving the doctors in Cardiff recently and, as I came out of the door, I walked straight into Binda, and I started crying and he looked at me horrified. I could see in his eyes that he saw a potentially dying man in front of him. But not yet flower, not yet, thank God!

I'm still too weak to walk far, and I still get asked, "Why did you go to work?" My answer is always the same: if I stayed in the house I'd be playing music and talking on the phone, which is exactly what I do at work. So there!

Buster's first public appearance

During May 2011, I was struggling to keep up appearances and continue with the many events I'd committed myself to. Throughout May, volunteers of the Tŷ Olwen Hospice had erected their annual tea tent at Clyne Gardens in Swansea to raise much-needed funds. I was honoured to open the event on what turned out to be a beautiful sunny Saturday morning. The setting was stunning with all the flowers in bloom. Taking of flowers, many of my local Garden members were in attendance, although I'm not certain they were there to see *me*. I had let it be known that I would be accompanied by Buster. He was such a hit with everyone. Some visitors even brought their own dogs to meet Buster, and he just adored being the centre of attraction. He loves all the attention and having his photograph taken. While I was doing all the official bits, Gabe and his mam, Peggy, were holding court and putting the world to rights with some of the Garden members.

To be honest, I was so ill that day; all I can really remember was that there were loads of people staring at me as if it was my last engagement and, to be honest, that's what it felt like.

I was given a cup of tea and I could hardy lift the cup, but Buster did the honours of opening the proceedings by tearing the ribbon into the refreshment tent and he was presented with his own gift bag for the occasion. He knew it was for him and immediately took the doggy blanket out of the bag!

That was a very hard day and that night Gabe searched everywhere to buy papaya fruit as someone told him it cured ulcers, but it didn't, and anyway, I quickly came to the conclusion that I didn't like papaya fruit, whichever way it was prepared. *Ych-a-fi!*

New management

I've never really had a manager, simply because I don't trust anyone to look after my career. However, one day, an actor friend of mine, Dan O'Gormane, suggested that I contact Dragon Personal Management which is based in Cardiff and London. So I took the plunge, or rather I had to get out of the shower because the phone kept ringing. Dan had approached them directly, passed on my number and their representative, Spencer, was calling from London to introduce himself. Well, from the moment that we started talking, we hit it off big time. I felt as if we'd known each other for years. We arranged to meet at the BBC one evening and we got on famously.

Spencer said that he wanted to represent me and I felt good about it. We met again and chatted and planned. We were learning about each other in the process, and I felt that I could trust this guy. I've lived a long time and have seen a lot of things. I knew this man and his company was right for me. As time went on he invited me to his house in Cardiff where I met his wife, Tammy. She too was terrific, and I felt right at home with them both.

We've also met on neutral territory. I invited Spencer up to Cwmafan and we ate at the Rolling Mill, of course. Even within the first few weeks, we'd established areas that I needed to address which had been ignored while I'd been so unwell.

Together with my friend, Sarah Barry Williams, we have set up a new website which we'll continue to develop.

Spencer has become an asset inasmuch as he is able to cast an independent eye on all correspondence. Instances of hate mail and abusive emails have virtually disappeared; they've been sorted out once and for all.

He now knows the areas that I excel in and my preferences, likes and dislikes, and he pushes my name in the appropriate circles. I particularly love working with choirs and I just go over the top with after dinner speaking. Spencer has also accepted my challenge to get me back performing at the Benidorm Palace – I think it's mainly because he wants to come out with me as my personal manager! Why not? He's now turned into one of my best friends. I can say anything to him and he'll stand by me, whatever. He's also a keen photographer and has taken numerous publicity shots for me. Spencer has done more for me in the year that I've been on his books than others had done for me throughout my whole life.

We also have a mutual love of Spain and, to hear him moan about the cold and wet weather on his return from the continent, you'd swear we were joined at the hip. He must have nerves of steel to manage me. I couldn't have found a better man to put up with me – at least Gabe gets a break! But this just goes to prove that there are a lot of good people out there, we just haven't met them yet. And that's just what my radio show is all about, finding the good in people.

Chapter 9

Biggest birthday bash for ages – March 2012

Everyone knows how much I love my birthdays, and I honestly thought I'd never see another one on a number of occasions.

Theatres have to be booked well in advance, so I must have had some premonition of a show; but it could quite easily have been Gabe holding my memorial concert. Fortunately not!

I'd arranged for some of my dearest friends to support me on my return to Swansea's Grand Theatre. This was a charity show and a variety event like no other.

On the stage were my stalwarts: the June Bois Dancers, Bruce Anderson and Samantha Link, the return of Garden favourite Dame Mandy Starr, international opera sensations Rebecca Evans and Mark Llewellyn Evans, his brother Wynne (Go Compare) Evans, and West End lead, Simon Bowman.

As I pulled into the theatre car park, I received a phone call from Rhydian Roberts, the *X Factor* finalist. He's such a genuine guy and – get a load of this – he asked if he could sing on my show that night! Well, I mean to say, how could I answer that one? It took one point five seconds to say yes please, and a further five seconds to organise a parking place for him. Before his entrance onto the stage, I introduced him as Buster's new dog walker and Buster dragged him on in front of a full house. The crowd went nuts, screaming and all sorts. My surprise guest star and the audience were just overwhelmed by his presence.

Mandy Starr's dream came true when she performed a duet with the acclaimed West End *Phantom of the Opera* performer,

Simon Bowman. Bruce and Rebecca sang a duet of a song they'd recently recorded together, Rebecca and Wynne danced and bickered like an old married couple – very Noel Coward! Carole Rees Jones made her first live performance as the Dorothy Squires Experience before the Garden that evening, all plumes and feathers and frocks and voice! The audience warmed to her immediately and made her their latest Garden favourite.

Also on the bill that evening were the South Wales Gay Mens' Choir. They were established in 2008 and I met them around that time when they were rehearsing at the BBC studios in Llandaff. I hit it off with the lads but wasn't certain if I met their criteria for becoming a member – as if! But I was honoured that they asked me to be a patron of the choir and, whenever possible, I attend their performances. I was delighted that they were able to perform at this event. They have an outstanding and varied repertoire and their presence was as colourful and as humorous as could only be expected – an all-round experience that the audience thoroughly enjoyed. I can only wish the lads every success as they continue to entertain.

I'm sure that people will never forget that evening – truly one of the best in show business history in Wales. To see so many talented stars and household names on one bill and holding the show together brilliantly, keeping everyone in order, making certain the correct music and backing tracks were played, stage managing and much more, was Gabe.

At the time, I was being filmed for a fly-on-the-wall documentary for S4C about my health issues and it chronicled my attending Harley Street for consultations, the build-up to the show and interviews with my friends backstage. The film ended memorably with the dancers performing to my opening number, and me entering the stage from the wings.

I'm now asked on a regular basis if I'm going to do another show at the Swansea Grand. The trouble is that that was a bit of a benchmark. Can I top the last one? Everybody says to me that I could, but I don't know. I think I'd like to have David

Emanuel on my next show; he's terrific on stage. Maybe I should go knocking doors again, the doors of the big stars. Well, to be honest, nobody has said no to me yet. Fingers crossed.

April 2012

Throat still bad. Struggling to talk. The voice comes and goes but the big thing is that I can't sing at all and I'm heartbroken. It's not as if I've been pushing things too much. Now pinning my hopes on a full recovery.

Being made homeless is on the agenda

A new problem: I might be made homeless in Cardiff. Why? A year-and-a-half ago I requested the installation of gas central heating in my flat from a national company. They carried out all the necessary checks on the building and legislation, and confirmed it was suitable to be installed into the property, a ground-floor flat. The work was done, with a couple of holes drilled into the outside wall for two pipes and an outflow, together with a box on the wall containing the reading meter. No different to any other properties in the area, in the country even.

We'd actually made enquiries a few years earlier, but the cost of installing gas into the building from the main road was extortionate and it wouldn't have been a private line. And any future installations into the building would've been taken from our mains line. Gabe had made further enquiries to the service agents of the property and was advised that they could not meet the cost, and any central heating installation would be our own choice and we'd have to meet the bill. So, we dropped the idea at that point. But, back in December 2010, when the weather was so cold, I made further enquiries and, with the new regulations and change in suppliers, installation was now more affordable.

I've now been contacted by the service agents who've said that I carried out the installation without permission. I've owned the property for 18 years – but I've had a warning advising me that I've altered the structure of my flat without permission and it also intimates that I've put other residents at risk and that our buildings' insurance is null and void. Basically, they want me to have the supply taken out, at my own cost, which leaves me with no central heating or hot water or cooking facilities – effectively making me homeless. If this was such an issue, why wasn't it picked up earlier in the past 18 months? They carry out enough inspections in the area. Apparently, someone on the committee objected to the pipes which, although regulation, stood out and were too noticeable! As for the insurance, well they'll just have to get the policy changed. I can't believe that gas central heating is a risk to the community! This has all been passed to my solicitor. I can't deal with this at the moment. I don't feel strong enough and, anyway, I physically don't have the voice to argue.

It's a Saturday night and I'm sat in the house in Cwmafan depressed because I can't sing. My voice is damaged and I'm trying to come to terms with the fact that I may never sing again – well, not like I used to. I feel sometimes that I want to die, as singing and entertaining isn't just a job but a way of life, and part of my life has been shot dead.

21 May 2012

It's a Monday and I'm rather tense as, on Thursday, I'm off again to Harley Street. I don't know if they can do anything to save my voice as it's sounding like sandpaper at the moment. I've not been able to sing for over a year and it's killing me. All these years of building myself up and gaining a bit of fame and filling theatres and it's all been taken away from me by tablets. My life is as bad now as it was at the start – heartbreaking. I'm struggling to talk on air, and if the radio went that would be the end of my life. I'll never trust anyone again as long as I live. I want my singing voice back at any cost. How can I get through the rest of my life knowing that I can never walk on a stage again and sing?

July 2012

I've just seen the Olympic opening ceremony. I enjoyed some of it. I don't think people will get it all, but hey, there you go, it's a spectacular!

I still can't sing and it hurts when I talk and my voice is still hoarse. I now feel in my heart that I'll never sing again. After all, there are some things that you know in life. I've been to Harley Street so many times now and nothing seems to be putting my condition right. I would like to continue broadcasting for Radio Wales, if my voice lasts.

↕

A couple of months ago my credit card company contacted me, checking some sales on my account and some clever git had bought a blow-up doll and charged it to me! I had the money back eventually, but I had to convince the credit card people that I hadn't bought the doll. I simply said, how could I? It was a woman doll. Not much use to me! And today I've checked my online bank statement and some firm has taken £254 out of my account. What's with this lousy world? It's all getting a bit too much for me.

↕

More agony. I fell downstairs the other day and broke two toes. They are nearly killing me. I'm a walking disaster area. And I know it's the last thing I should be doing but I've been trying on shoes galore. Can you believe that since I've been ill and lost all that weight, I've also lost a size and a half in shoes. Honest! I don't think I've ever heard of that before, but I'm the living proof. Now that makes me believe that anything is possible!

I'm so glad that I've met and befriended Carole Rees Jones. She really is a true friend to me. I would have gone off the deep end without her. She often stays with me and gives me a lot of confidence. She also buys me Spanish soap. She knows what makes me tick. I ask her how I'm ever going to get through my life without being able to perform on stage.

They're now talking about putting collagen injections into my vocal cords but I've just been watching a TV programme about big mistakes using collagen. My God, what if it made things worse? As if things could get any worse. Gabe has been doing research, too. He is concerned that collagen and Botox injections are only a temporary solution and, once the effect wears off, you have to endure further treatment. Not happy, but need to check further with my specialist.

I'm in the shop today for Gabe as he has gone to see his mam in Cardiff. I'm ready for the 20 questions brigade.

The heavens have just opened and it's so bad that customers are congregating in the shop until the rain stops. They'll be here forever then. I find it very therapeutic watching the crushed ice turning round and round in the slush puppy machine.

It's Sunday night and I'm in tears. My world has fallen apart. I've tried some basic vocal exercises and my voice just gave out. I can't sing and people around me treat me as if I've just dropped a cup on the floor. I don't know what I'm going to do. I'm sat in the house on the weekends when I should be out performing on stage, and it's pissing down with rain. A whole weekend like a tsunami. It never lets up. I need to see my specialist but it's too hectic to go to London because of the Olympics and the hotels have quadrupled in price all because of poxy sport. I'm crawling up the wall right now. I'm missing Benidorm as well, as I've lost my work out there, too. My God, if I saw that doctor who gave me those tablets I'd run him over. Buster has just come to see me and has given me a *cwtch* (cuddle) and he makes me feel good. He loves me and the treats that I give him. There are a lot of people looking into my medical situation at the moment and all I want is to be able to sing again.

People can be kind, especially on the radio. Radio is different to everyday life at home or on the street – always special.

A few days ago I attended an audition to find a lookalike to appear instead of me in a play, because of my voice problems. My God, it was weird seeing actors trying to impersonate me.

The centenary of the Llwydcoed Brass Band, St Tydfil's Church, Merthyr Tydfil, August 2012

I have the honour of being president of the Llwydcoed Brass Band and I've been invited to compere their show at St Tydfil's Church. I wasn't sure if I could do it as I was still unwell. At least, on the radio I couldn't be seen. But the band was celebrating a century of entertaining audiences and I knew I couldn't let them down.

While I received such a warm welcome from everyone, it was Buster who stole the show holding attendance outside, with Garden members queuing to see him and have their pictures taken with him. It put a huge smile on my face, I can tell you.

The show began and Buster was initially quite content to lie down beside Gabe in the church and listen to the singers and the band, but it was obvious he wasn't fussed about the drummer. I think Buster thought it was becoming a bit too noisy for him, so Gabe took him out for a walk about the town. I was 'at home' in the pulpit that evening, but thank goodness there was a microphone, otherwise I'd not have been heard. I couldn't sing, but just about managed to host the event, announcing the songs and tunes in between, and a couple of jokes here and there. I felt safe in the pulpit.

The audience were somewhat fascinated with me and quite a few were bold enough to ask me how far my cancer had developed. I kept repeating the same thing, that I didn't have cancer at all. I got away with 'the voice' that evening, and it gave me a bit of confidence to carry on. Most importantly I was privileged to be at such a fantastic evening which formed part of St Tydfil's festival.

We take Buster just about everywhere with us. He's so funny. As we leave Cwmafan, he starts getting chatty in the car. It's almost as if he's trying to talk. Then, once we are out of Cwmafan, he quietens down somewhat. He likes the window open a bit so he can stick his tongue out of the car, but he's not too keen on the window being open too much. When we get towards Cardiff Bay and he recognises areas he knows, he starts chattering again. And as we get towards Gabe's mam's house, you just can't stop him. He gets so excited; he knows he's going to get spoilt rotten. As if we don't spoil him enough!

↕

Since being ill for some 16 months, I continue to have trouble breathing. I don't know what to feel at the moment, but anger is very prominent. I want to lash out at the man who has taken my singing career away from me. I tried doing an after dinner speech and failed miserably. I kept losing my voice every other minute. If I lost the radio I would die.

I'm watching so much sport at the moment that people think I'm cracking up. In particular the *La Vuelta Ciclista a España* and I'm totally infatuated with seeing the Spanish roads and countryside. I'm absolutely mesmerised and it's making me happy one minute, then sad the next.

Carole Rees Jones has just called to tell me that's she's bought some air tickets for next month for Benidorm and I have to go. What a girl. So I'm off, and bugger everything else.

↕

I'm sat in the shop for Gabe to go to the Cash & Carry and I wonder how my mother managed to run it. She must have worked her butt off in this shop. Lord knows, Gabe is permanently knackered and I try to do whatever I can to help him. At night I'm interviewing Rhydian Roberts or Rebecca Evans and the following day I'm weighing spuds or cleaning the shop – but that's me. I love it, and I would do anything for Gabe, he's special. He's my number one – after Buster, that is!

Another person has just popped in the shop and told me that they've lost their job. How do you handle that situation? It would kill me. I've worked my whole life, paid mortgages and now what would they be worth if I sold up – that's if I could sell up. People can't earn enough to survive and this upsets me so much.

I'm waiting for a call from Harley Street – nothing as yet. Two doctors are working together to see what would be the best for me throat-wise. Still can't sing.

September 2012

The year is almost three-quarters through already. I just can't believe I'm still as bad this far in as I was at the beginning of the year. We've just finished doing a show in Porthcawl and it was a great success, but I couldn't sing, so I won't be doing any more until something gives with my throat. People say, "Oh, but you can do comedy," but I don't want to. I want to be able to sing again, perform fully and if I can't, that's that – it's the end for me. I had my old team around me: the lovely Dame Mandy Starr, Bruce Anderson, Samantha Link, Carole Rees Jones and the June Bois Dancers, and my special guest star of the evening, my old trooper, driving all the way from Anglesey, Tammy Jones. They were all fabulous, but I had to stand in the wings and watch everyone else sing all their favourite songs and I couldn't and it was bloody killing me. The charity will now lose out because of this situation, as well as myself.

The Olympics have finished now, thank God. Even I've had enough. I'm still waiting for summer, nothing as yet, just more flooding.

I took a friend, Jason, to the hospital the other day as he

wasn't able to get an emergency GP appointment. While he was waiting to be seen, I checked my emails, caught up on a few phone calls and had a cup of tea etc. Well, a five-hour wait and you'd start to get bored, too. Don't forget, I wouldn't have had time later as I have to prepare for work. Besides, I needed to go to the loo, too! Anyway, off to the café at the hospital I go. I got into the revolving doors that were moving around at the time, as they do. I stepped in and the doors stopped and locked me in. People were pointing and laughing for about ten minutes and just thought that I was being filmed. Three engineers tried for a while to get me out and, after about 20 minutes, they did manage it. But I did start to go crazy; I thought I was losing it. I was worried in case they couldn't release me in time for work. When I was eventually released, an old woman asked me how did I get in there and, sarcastically, I replied that the revolving doors just pulled up outside my house and picked me up and brought me down to the hospital.

I've been back over to Gabe's shop this morning. Saw Jason for a catch-up. So many people just popping back and forth, just for a chat – the tales are incredible. It's getting to be like a surgery for my radio show. I can't get over how many people wear their pyjamas, slippers and dressing gowns out on the streets. These aren't onesies, but actual bed wear. I hope it's not turning into the village equivalent of *The Jeremy Kyle Show*. My mother would turn in her grave.

↕

I remember when I was about 17 years old, one of my school friends, Wendy, asked me to give her a lift to Swansea to buy some new platform shoes. The shoes turned out to be like stilts and she wore them out of the shop. She stumbled, tumbled and tripped up the street as she wasn't used to them. So she asked me to steady her by putting her arm in mine. It felt strange and some people I knew saw us together and started making comments like, "How can that poof pull a smart girl like that?"

People then and now can't leave me alone. I always ask myself the question, "What is my life to do with you?" I was born too soon. I'd have more of a chance now as a young gay man rather than me at my age now.

↕

I'm always racking my brain for questions for my radio programme. I can't simply ask a question on pop music or history because you'd only have to go on the Internet and Bob's your uncle. So I have to have a question that was personal to me or my family or a friend, such as, "What do you think my mother did next?" etc. The trouble is that I forget the questions unless I write them down immediately.

↕

I'm trying to come to terms with not being able to sing. If I try to sing it sounds rough and coarse and usually, within ten minutes, I lose my voice completely. But, I've decided I need to perform. I'll just have to get back out there and do a different type of show – more piano, funnier stories, little chats with the audience like I do on the phone on my radio show. I've missed the stage so much after 18 months of doing nothing. How could I let someone destroy me like this?

Buster has just come in to see me in the front room. He knows when I'm on a downer. He's such a comfort. He gives nothing but love. During the day you can often see him sitting in the front bedroom window looking out. People calling at the shop often remark about him watching their every move. I tell them he's not being nosey, just concerned!

Someone stopped me in the street in Neath and asked me how my mother was. So I just said it out loud, "Still dead, thank you" (there was a bit of hurt and jealousy there on my part).

I often think that if I'd been a better son my mother would have lived longer, but I could do no more. I did everything I could. I wish she could have had a better life, not worrying about me and watching out for me and protecting me. But hey, my relationship has done better that most people's. Me and Gabe intend to get hitched and we've been to get a licence, but I can't find it – sad or what!

I've just phoned the registry office in Cardiff and sorted it. We can get hitched and all we have to do is set a date. Fancy getting married and I'm nearly a pensioner (in leather trousers).

I remember once a neighbour had retired from a job at the hospital and, as a friendly prank, the hospital staff made a man's willy out of Plaster of Paris and stuck it on the front of my neighbour's car. I heard a commotion outside the shop and there were crowds of people screaming, with cameras flashing. You've guessed it. There was my mother right in the middle holding this willy as if it was an Oscar. And people think I'm wild. I'm like a bloody nun next to my mother.

Christmas is just around the corner and I dread it. It hurts me so much for dozens of reasons. Gabe says I should try and enjoy it, but I'd rather ban it. The thought of paper hats and everything full of sugar. It drives me mental. I can't help it. If I'm honest, I didn't have the happiest of times growing up and Christmas meant that my tormentor would be calling at the house and I lived in fear of being abused further. At Gabe's I see all the decorations and the table is laid out like a film set and I watch them opening their presents. I know I'm part of it but it's all too much and far too late for me to fully enjoy. To me, I like to be at work – I usually am – because so many lonely people rely on the wireless for company and I've been told that they get reassurance that everything is OK if I'm about. Otherwise, I love all the movies and TV specials on the telly at Christmas. That's me sorted – Gabe's mam's dinner, my radio show and a selection of my favourite telly programmes that I recorded earlier.

Christmas Night, 2012

I'm listening to my own radio show. It may seem like the easy option to record a show ahead of time but it takes far longer to arrange guests to phone in or record interviews, especially the week before Christmas. But we did invite our listeners to record short messages to be included, as well. So it's a treat for me not to be working tonight, don't you think? I'm really enjoying the show and hope everyone else is, too. I've had a wonderful dinner with Peggy, Gabe's mam, as always, and now I'm fit for dropping. This Christmas has been so damn hard coping with my throat problems. I've missed going out entertaining. After all, that's what I do.

January 2013

I'm just sitting in the front room in Cwmafan and Buster is lolling on the chesterfield like Zsa Zsa Gabor. *Dancing on Ice* has just started and Gareth Thomas has opened the show and done really well. I think I've discovered what's keeping me from getting back really well again. The wet weather. Dear God, I've never seen (or heard) so much rain, wind and destruction. What have we done to deserve this? And it's even taking my concentration off the box.

↕

Louise has been a godsend these past few months, and breezed into our lives, not so much like Mary Poppins on a cloud, but more like a tornado! She was introduced to us by another friend, Sharon, who worked for the local newspaper. My first impression was that she looked a right bloody handful, but then I wasn't my usual self and not liking anyone at the time.

The main thing was that she and Gabe seemed to hit it off, and she started helping him out in the shop on an ad hoc basis. I have to be honest, she's turned out to be perfect; she gets along with everyone and knows how to handle the kids. A huge plus

Gabe and me, the happy couple on our special day, 7 March 2013

Rebecca Evans and Only Men Aloud performing at the wedding of the year!

A day to remember: Li Harding, me, Sarah Barry Williams, Carole Rees Jones and Gabe

Linda Jenkins, me and Toni Carol

With Emyr Wyn

'Baby, It's Cold Outside' – singing a duet with Gillian Elisa

With Sue Roderick

With Ieuan Rhys

With Deiniol Wyn Rees

With Peter Karrie and Carole Rees Jones

With Carole Rees Jones and Bruce Anderson

The June Bois Dancers

Singing a duet with Tammi Bois

Always a tower of strength, my dear friend Teddi Munro performing at one of my charity events

With Welsh songstress, Diane Cousins

With Tammi Bois in rehearsal

With talented Welsh actress and author, Liz Williams

With Only Boys Aloud, backing Bonnie Tyler to win the Eurovision

With the charming Lynn Bowles of Radio 2 fame

With old family friend, broadcaster Graham Jenkins, brother of Richard Burton

With X Factor's Rhydian Roberts

Me and my double, Jonathan Millard

With broadcaster Wynne Evans

Welsh comedy actor, former Flying Picket and good mate, Brian Hibbard

At the British Heart Foundation (Wales) charity evening with BBC Wales weather presenter, Behnaz Akhgar

Caught 'out shopping' with Rebecca Evans

Best mates with West End star, Simon Bowman

Charity fundraising with the Pearly Kings and Queen(s) of London

Me and Paddington Bear – guess where we are!

Recording *Come the Revolution* with Chris Corcoran

Supporting Shân Cothi with her charity events

Beverley Humphreys hosting 'A Night at the Musicals' at The Orangery

Me with the ever so versatile Miss Tina Sparkle who dropped in when broadcasting on Radio Cymru

With Meyrick and Irene Sheen, parents of Michael
(Photo: Geoffrey Akhurst)

With Kelvin Guy, CEO and founder of Gŵyl Ffilm Bae Caerfyrddin – Carmarthen Bay Film Festival Community Group
(Photo: Geoffrey Akhurst)

Gabe and me backstage at the BBC Swansea Big Bash broadcast

With friend and comedienne, Wendy Kane

Rehearsing for a cameo role in Mal Pope's musical, *Cappuccino Girls*

With Helen Enser Morgan at rehearsals for the musical, *Cappuccino Girls*

With my Garden flowers at Porthcawl Grand Pavilion

Ceri Dupree entertaining my Garden at Porthcawl

Unmasked: Wales's Phantom, Peter Karrie entertaining the audience

On stage at Porthcawl
Grand Pavilion

Nice tie! Backstage at Porthcawl

Gabe, ready to operate the microwave! (Assistant Sound Engineer at the Porthcawl show)

With Jack, our local Olympic Torch carrier and his family

There must be a
camera about!
Buster Llŷr
posing at home

Buster in his dressing room and 'resting' between appearances

Gabe and Buster relaxing at home

Delphi – guide dog and companion for the afternoon at a guide dogs' event in Cardiff

Delphi and demonstrator, Andrew, preparing me

What an experience!

Mission completed!

Much-needed supporters,
volunteers and puppy walkers

Early years

The Jersey years – with one of my fans

At the Waikiki Club with my Jersey fans – eh!

My working clothes

Gabe back in the studios broadcasting

Recuperating in Spain – no talking allowed!

At my happiest, performing at the piano

Gabe learning his lines for the play, *Encore*

Strictly Come Dancing – outside the Pineapple Studios, London

Gabe cleaning my boat, Jake

In the studio, waiting for the news to finish

Having a boogie on a Friday!

point is that she knows them or their parents, so nothing gets past her. She's turned out to be a cracking friend to us both, and me and her are so alike in our sense of humour, ideas, and just about everything. Biggest thing is that she's probably one of the most trustworthy persons I've met. Believe you me, you don't get many of them in a pound! She's also been a great help in re-establishing the charity following my illness, attending my concerts and selling the merchandise, and preparing the shop for the re-launch. In fact, I've never quite met a family like Louise's. They support each other and I envy that. I'm not that keen that her husband Karl keeps snakes, so I won't be visiting them often, but their husky, Nanooke, is just adorable, and their two boys, Morgan and Tom, are just wonderful – and love listening to me on Radio Wales, so they tell me!

Looking back at the shop when my mother had it, my God, she was one crazy woman. She always said that she should have plenty of stock, just in case of snow or war. She had so many chocolates in cases that they ended up under the beds, on top of the wardrobe and anywhere else that she could put them, even in neighbours' houses. She would weigh potatoes on an old set of scales, the ones with pound weights you piled on the side until the bucket with potatoes moved upwards. I have to admit that all the bags of spuds were different weights because someone would come in and start talking to her and weights and measures went out the window. I remember an old lady from across the road coming into her shop and asking for one pound of potatoes, and could my mother make them big ones!

My mother had a traveller (sales rep) call to see her with greetings cards and he was so cheap that people flocked to buy her cards. The traveller wouldn't dare sell his cards to another shop locally, as my mother always cooked him a dinner to get the best deal.

↕

I'm sat here typing away like a good one and the pain in my legs is horrendous. Don't ever get diabetes, it's a swine. Most days I can't walk a stone's throw. Stairs are a killer. But I shall battle on as I always do. People still stare at the way I walk, but there you go – so many aliments, I tend to focus on the one that causes me the greatest pain or problem at the time.

It's Sunday night and Gabe is watching some cowing crap on the telly. So I'm getting on with some more writing.

But we did manage to see Owen Money this weekend at the Princess Royal Theatre in *Babes in the Wood*. Tammi Bois was in it as well and, fair play, it was really good. The children loved Owen and he has a wonderful rapport with the little ones. It's good to see traditional family entertainment on stage which introduces youngsters to the theatre. I hope that they enjoyed it enough to want to return, not just as children but as they get older, too.

Tomorrow's another day and I wonder what this week will bring. I can never tell. I've been so concerned about my health lately as I'm having really bad chest pains which stops me from doing anything at all. Sometimes I don't have the strength to put my phones on charge. I don't have the energy to stoop down and pick something up. I've seen my GP and he's given me tablets but he wants to see me again in a few days.

I need to have the marriage civil ceremony with Gabe as I don't know what the future holds for me and I want all the loose ends tied up, just to feel at ease.

I'm convinced that my days are numbered due to the illness I suffered as a result of the drugs and, of course, the damn diabetes. I don't mind dying, just as long, as I've said, my ashes are scattered in Spain as I never want to come back here. Not to suffer name calling, abuse and crap weather. If I don't see the UK again it will be too soon.

Carole Rees Jones has just come back from her villa in Spain. Why she comes back here I'll never know.

↕

Eddie May was the manager of Cardiff Football Club and, when we met one evening at a charity do, I learnt he was a bit of a fan of mine and the programme. As time went on he'd call at the local club to see me playing keyboards and we'd chat and we got to know each other really well. Eddie supported me in all my charity bashes. He would even pick me up in his car and take me to charity shows and sporting events. He took me to meet the team once and to a few of their matches. I even got to know some of the players and a few things about footy. Eddie was never put off being seen with me as some others are. I was just Chris Needs on the radio and not Chris Needs the gay. Eddie May was a massive name in sport and he raised my profile a lot by introducing me to top names in the business.

As is always the case in entertainment, you drift apart due to commitments and just keep in touch once in a while by phone. When news broke that Eddie May had died, I was gutted. I hadn't seen him for a while and I wished I'd kept more in touch with him. I will never forget Eddie for his kindness and, perhaps more, for his acceptance.

Chapter 10

The wedding of the year

I'd never wanted to be married, being 'one of them'. It had never crossed my mind but, now, I find myself in a totally different world. I've been with Gabe for over 23 years and it's solid. We're both happy in our own strange ways. But since the death of my mother and her 'will', I find myself minus a family. Sad, but that's it. There's nothing I can do about it. If I was to give them money, it would be like buying a family member and I know that's wrong. I don't want my non-speaking family to be my next of kin. So, a while back, we applied for a civil ceremony licence and got it with a view to getting hitched. But, when I was taken ill, it was shelved. One day I checked the expiry date on the licence and it had three days to run. I asked the registrar could I extend the date and the reply was "No, not possible." So, I asked what could I do and she said why not get married in three days' time. Well, why the hell not? Neither of us wanted a lavish affair. We didn't panic and just called a few friends and had about a dozen celebs come along, too. Gabe called into the apartments to collect my Spanish suit and dropped in to see his mum. Unfortunately his brother was working away, and his sister couldn't get leave at such short notice.

We were good to go on 7 March 2013, at City Hall, Cardiff, at three o'clock. Gabe was working at the shop until midday and then Louise agreed to cover. She also arranged for our buttonholes, beautiful yellow roses. Sharon accompanied us to Cardiff, stopping off at Tesco's, Culverhouse Cross, to pick up Carole Rees Jones. She'd cancelled her trip to Spain, jumped in the back of the car and proceeded to change her clothes as we carried on to City Hall. Rebecca Evans was there waiting with Only Men Aloud and scattered celebs. My opening line, "After today Buster is not a bastard."

Gabe and me were taken into an anteroom by the registrar to fully explain the proceedings etc., while the guests were assembled in the main ceremony room. As we entered Only Men Aloud started to sing and we walked into gasps and applause and, my God, my emotions started going haywire. We stood and faced the registrar and the words started flowing, "We are gathered here today..." My nerves were getting the better of me at this stage.

Then we heard the phrase, "Does anyone know of any reason why these people should not be joined together?" Everyone turns to look about, just like in a movie, and Li Harding catches my eye and sings, "It should have been me." That restored me to normality, briefly.

I crumbled when I was asked to "...turn and face your partner and repeat these words." I couldn't. I was a total mess. I fluffed the words big time. I probably sounded as if I'd just been dragged out of a terrible accident. I somehow got through it and turned to look at the people and they were all teary. Gabe, on the other hand, was very cool and professional and word-perfect.

Carole Rees Jones was amazing. She filmed it and took photos galore after the ceremony. We were thrilled that so many friends were able to join us at such short notice. We had no reception as we wanted to get back to Buster as soon as possible, because we were off to work later that evening. So at five o'clock, I was in my pants cooking fish fingers and mash potatoes, while Gabe was hoovering through the house and, afterwards, cashing up and preparing the till for the morning. We had a kip and went to work, knackered. And then I told the world of our special news.

What a lucky boy I am, being accepted by the lovely Gabe, and me an old damaged crock. And our song is now 'One Hand,

One Heart' from the show *West Side Story*. We'll never forget the performances of Only Men Aloud and Rebecca Evans – it was just incredible.

19 March 2013

I played the new Bonnie Tyler Eurovision song last night and bragged her up to the heavens, like I always do. She'd been on *The One Show* in London and was on the M4 coming back to Wales and heard me play the song. She phoned me straight away. I called her back and we chatted on air for ages. She is such a true friend to me. We met when we were both teenagers and we are still best friends. The support she gives me and my radio show is immense. We laughed and laughed on the radio and that's good for people to hear. We all need a damn good laugh in these days of doom and gloom.

I'm rubbing shoulders with top stars most days and it's still an incredible feeling. I love my celebrity friends and they must think the world of me as they jump in a minute if I ask them to do something for me.

I'm writing this in the shop that used to be my mother's. I'm doing two hours for Gabe so that he can go to the Cash & Carry. It's not much different to the radio to be honest, as people are popping in and having a quick chat about whatever and then off they go again. Some just come in for a bloody good moan and I can't blame them. Today, John Brown, an old customer of my mother's, popped in to pick up a few things. We reminisced over old times when my mother used to serve him. My God, he told me some wonderful stories of times past. He used to live on his own behind my mother's house and she thought the world of him. He's still a really nice guy to this day and doesn't look any different. Thank you, John.

↕

Since this horsemeat scandal, I'm completely off meat. What's happened to British standards? No such thing as far as I'm concerned. What a waste of time this country has become. Now at the moment I'm listening to the news and they say we might be running out of gas supplies. Have you ever heard so much nonsense in your life? What about North Sea gas? Was that a fairy tale or is some country siphoning off our gas and warming their butts in front of their fires? I was asked the other day, are you Welsh or British? Neither, I said, I'm European; the weather's nicer there. That's my story, so I'm sticking to it.

I was looking for a new car online; nothing immediate just something for a few months time. I'm fancying one of those little Fiat 500 – they look so trendy, retro and foreign. Then this woman said to me (as I was in the shop), "It's all right for people like you, celebrity status." So I said to her, well if you like it that much, why don't you become one, too? So jealous.

I think the Garden 'album of the week' tonight is André Rieu – he'll transport me abroad. This will be a good week for me.

Going to town with my mother in the car was an experience

I'd be sat in the front of the car and my mother would be driving. Then, as she approached the local bus stop, she'd say to me, "Play up and wave your hands in the air." So I would and, as she passed the bus stop, she'd give me a slap around the head and shout at me. Then she'd explain that she'd seen a woman at the bus stop and my mother didn't want to stop to pick her up. So I was a distraction and she'd missed who was at the bus stop. Then she'd add, "I don't like her, she always wins at the bingo."

The horse out the front

My mother was crossing the road from the shop over to the house, and she noticed a horse trotting down the main road. Then the horse did a massive poo in the middle of the road. It was everywhere. My mother ran in the house and shouted,

"Harold, come quick, a horse has just dropped its guts on the road." Now my father, being a keen gardener, ran and fetched a bucket and shovel and, while my mother stopped the traffic, my father shovelled up the manure of a lifetime. He kept it in the shed for a while and it stunk for weeks, even after moving it down to the allotment.

↕

I feel bad sometimes when I speak to Scottish people because, some of the time, I can't understand them. Anyway, one day I was watching a Scottish TV programme called *Countryside 999* and it made me feel a bit better about this situation; they had subtitles when the patients spoke from the hooose (house). I have the same trouble with Liverpudlians – very difficult to understand.

↕

We've had terrible cold weather so far in 2013. It's been so bad, it's embarrassing. People say to me in Porthcawl how sorry they are to have come to Wales for their holidays because of the weather, and I tell them it's OK for them, they've only got to put up with it for a week – we've got a lifetime of it.

A chap just walked into the shop and said to me, "I've never met a millionaire before," and stared at me. So I said, "Nor have I, love."

Gabe's gone to the doctors today about his tablets for his blood pressure; he's been prescribed various medications but he's had a bad reaction to all he's taken. His legs and feet have ballooned since he's been on these particular pills. Funny, where have I heard that before?

I've just put out a question on the radio which was, "What three things have I got to do before I die?" Answers: Live in Spain; go to an Eurovision Song Contest and visit Southfork Ranch in Dallas. Will it ever happen? I doubt it very much.

I've never seen so much doom and gloom about this world.

I was watching Kim Jong-un, the new ruler of North Korea. He's inherited a brutal regime from his father and refuses so far to make any positive changes. He's expressing his desire to expand his realm and, given the current lack of resistance, he could succeed. I couldn't believe what I saw last year, at the 2012 Olympics, when the South Korean flag was flown in error. When those from North Korea came out onto the field they started crying, they were terrified. His own people! I suppose they might get a bit more than a bollocking if they didn't show how upset they were. If they flew the Spanish flag when I walked out instead of the British one, I'd be bloody thrilled. I'd start dancing and chanting, "I wish, I wish."

I love my show more than ever now that I've got Llinos Jones, my favourite producer in the world. She does everything for me and more. I'm so lucky to have her. I don't want her ever to go, and she's in demand as far as I can tell; she does quite a bit for Radio 4, too. There's posh for you. I remember being on stage with Alex Jones from *The One Show* and I said to her, "What's it like working in London with running water and electricity." She took it brilliantly. It was a great night. My God, she's done well for herself, and rightly so!

I'm hoping this year to take my boat out as I've been trying to do so for five years now. The weather has been too bad (hard to believe) and there are no lay-bys out there at sea if it gets too rough! It's a sports boat and, boy, does it move! It has a double bedroom, toilet and lovely white leather seats. I'm hoping we might get some half-decent, second-hand weather. Why is the weather so bad here in Britain I'm asked everyday? Sometimes I wonder if it's because there are so many bad people here.

A woman asked me on my programme if I'd like a *cwtch* with her as she was lonely. I told her straight, "The homosexual is not for turning." I did like Maggie's campness.

I keep looking out of the window and hoping one day it will be hot like abroad. I'm a dreamer.

I was watching the London Marathon on TV the other day and the presenter said it was warming up in London, the skies were blue with not a cloud in the sky. I then looked out of the window here and saw massive black clouds. I thought there was a tsunami approaching.

I was destined for better parts. Gabe is looking at houses in Gibraltar to buy. I thought to myself, I won't stand in your way. You wouldn't see my arse for dust.

I've been having a run of bad luck in the studio in Llandaff, Cardiff, with the lousy computer. You probably know what I'm going to say, you've more than likely heard about it. For weeks, the computer that plays the music kept dying, and would stop in the middle of the song and, more embarrassingly, in the middle of the news jingle; thank goodness the newsreader was Kim Marks – we've worked together for years and she battled through. Nobody seemed to be able to put their finger on the fault but I did come close to throwing it out of the window one night. It's sort of OK right now, but I'm not holding my breath.

I'm going to Cardiff a little early tonight to drop off my VAT returns with my accountant. What an exciting life I have! Pouring rain, as usual. I'm going to take a break in a minute and have a look at the prices of flights to Alicante – anything to get out of this nightmare.

Life seems the same at the moment. Get up, inject, cook breakfast for Gabe, do a little writing, dodge the rain, watch *Dallas*, cook tea, watch *Pointless* and then *Eggheads*, have an hour on the bed, then a bath and then to work. When I drive to work I think up questions for the show about me, my mam or whatever, and then pull the car to the side of the road and send the questions via email on my phone because if I don't I'll forget them by the time I get to the studios.

I've been suffering from a hoarse voice for past few weeks. I naturally put it down to the onset of a cold, bearing in mind the awful weather of late. But Gabe has come to the rescue once again. I'd forgotten to tell him that my GP had prescribed blood pressure tablets. Gabe knew exactly which ones I'd been given and told me it was one of the side effects (again!). I then looked these up and, lo and behold, Gabe was right. There it was confirmed, it said that the tablets can cause hoarseness. Can you imagine giving me those bloody tablets after what I've been through and the scars in my throat. Never again will I take a tablet unless I've studied it first.

$$\updownarrow$$

I always said that this would be the last book I'd ever write, but I might be swayed to do another.

I've lived and worked in 16 different countries and loved every moment of it. Where do I start?

Sweden was nice – very liberal and cool. No comments about sexuality, unlike here. (Mind you, nothing in the world is like here for destroying people.) Cold, but the people were nice.

Netherlands was ace. So free and easy in all sorts of ways, and everyone was so welcoming. I met a lovely girl who was a prostitute and she taught me Dutch. We met every morning for coffee, which is a religion there, and she would teach me her language and, in return, I would teach her Spanish. People must have thought it mighty strange her speaking to me in Dutch and me answering her in Spanish. Although, having said that, it didn't matter out there. But back here in Britain, we would've been stared at more than ever. She would then toddle off with her Marigolds (gloves) and clean the dungeon floors at the establishment she worked. She said the work, whatever it was, kept her children in a good education and nice house. I used to tell her a few Welsh words also, like the word for 'lady parts'… 'my Mary Jones' – work that one out for yourself!

I once worked in a rubber club in Berlin. Rubber is lovely, my mother used to say: you don't have to iron or press it!

Chapter 11

25 April 2013

When I left for the studio last night, I felt so low. But travelling back after such a good show, I feel happier, content and a lot stronger because I've come to a decision. If I'm to start planning my future, I need to downsize desperately. I'm putting my boat for sale, and my grand piano, as well as my caravan and the shops. In fact, everything except my mam's house. I'm going to live in the sun – a bit late in life, but I'm downsizing and that's the end of that. All I have to do now is tell Gabe. I'm bloody well out of here. Goodbye. My God, I feel good. I'll get Carole Rees Jones to sell my stuff for me. I can't wait to be away and make a new life for me and Gabe (and Buster!).

↕

There are a few things going on at the moment. A telly series is on the cards and a national TV programme about me and the Garden success. It will be on a national station so you never know I might get Radio 2 yet. I've always had the feeling that whatever I've tried, in the past and even now, I'm being scrutinised and studied with dismay because I'm camp.

I hope I get something on the network because that's a personal ambition and I'll keep nagging and knocking doors till it happens. If not, it's Spain and that's good enough for me any day.

I've told Gabe that I want to leave Wales and I think he's relieved for me. He knows what I've been put through over the years.

29 April 2013

Still coughing like a good 'un! Those tablets haven't left my system yet.

I said to Carole Rees Jones the other day, just after she'd dyed her hair, "Are you worried that you'll not be seen from outer space?" God, I had to shield my eyes!

The charity shop was broken into and a few thousand pounds' worth of stock and money has been taken. I'm so hurt as I've worked my butt off for years just to raise a bit to help others. I won't go on about this now as I'm so angry that I might say something I'll regret.

One thing is for sure, I have to leave Wales and just sit in the sun and let the rest of the world go by. That's a certainty. I've been looking at places in Benidorm and, my God, the prices are so low. This world is at an all-time low. They say there's no money, so where has it gone? Have the Martians come down here and taken it? I think something's got to give soon as people, as I've just experienced, are having to steal to survive.

I've just received a box of Manuka honey of the purest/highest rating. I've never liked it, but I've been swayed to try it and it does help a lot. So I'm buying it online as it's an expensive item.

Great, I'm going to Benidorm with Carole Rees Jones to view an apartment and I can't wait. I'm going to ask my boss if I can do my programme from Spain because others do, so why not me? I keep looking online at pictures of Spain and, to be honest, it's the only thing that keeps me going. My friend, Wendy Kane, is back out in Benidorm and I'm so happy for her, and it's what I want for me as well.

↕

When I started at the Beeb I was small fry in the shadow of the big boys. Now I feel as if I've cracked it and I have what I want. The company that now produces my show, Terrier Productions, treats me like royalty and I bloody love it. I've longed for this moment and I've got it. Nobody is taking my Llinos away from me. I never thought the day would come that I'd fight to keep a woman. But I will. I now look forward to going into work when I know who's there when I get in.

The hills are alive with the sound of bums being grazed!

As children we always went to Tips Gwyn, a man-made hill of lime waste covered with grass. We would slide down the hillside on a piece of cardboard which usually came from the Co-op – that's if we spoke nicely to Mr Davies, the Co-op manager. So many times I would slide into the stinging nettles. It was bloody awful. The injuries I sustained from sliding were blamed for the cuts to my bottom, but really it was my abuser who'd had his way with me. I always remember those words, "If there are no complications Margaret, nothing will go on his record. We'll keep it out of chapel." It was an awful time. I used to sit on the hillside and hide from this man, wishing that a spaceship would land to take me away, anywhere. This feeling has never left me. Some folk say, "Oh, Chris Needs and his tales of woe." But none of it was my fault. It was the fault of *that* adult and the other adults standing by and letting it happen. I made a den to hide in and that was a godsend. It saved me lots of times. I've often wondered, of late, if I hadn't been so ill these last two years, would I have been focusing so much on these events in my past so much. I can't shift them from my mind. I just can't bury these memories any more. They just keep surfacing.

And the memories of Copper Row, Cwmafan, have become more vivid as well. We had an outside toilet up the back garden where millions of brambles grew. Every time I went for a pee, I was scagged by those damn brambles. I was forever picking dock leaves to rub on my legs as a sort of natural cure for cuts, stings and bites. I can also smell the carbolic soap to this day; my dad would acquire it from the steelworks and cut up newspaper and place it on a hook behind the door. If we ran out of tomato ketchup, my mother would put vinegar in the bottle and shake the living daylights out of it. Then there'd be enough to have a bit on the plate. Clever mother!

There was a chapel at the end of the street, Tabor Chapel, a pretty building where they filmed *How Green Was My Valley*, with all the big Welsh names acting in it. At the other end of the street was a shop called Sammy's and he had a great business selling things from food to washing machines – the lot. There were, I think, at least four Co-ops in Cwmafan, a Lloyds Bank, a petrol station, insurance offices, a chip shop and mobile butcher and vegetable vans. Corner shops galore, piano teachers, a garage to mend the cars, a railway station… In fact, we never had to go out of the village. And, as I've said, the Betterware man, Mr Morris, used to call with cleaning stuff and he always gave me a free sample of shoe polish.

↕

At the moment I'm studying my condition with online medical experts just to see what's what. I need to understand why I was given those tablets. If I understand the reason, maybe I can understand why I nearly died. I still get nightmares about the state I was in. Seven stones in eight weeks. People stop me in the supermarket and say the usual, "How are you?" and I then make the decision whether to give an honest answer or a press release. If I go for the truth I tell them I'm still unwell, lost seven stones in eight weeks, can't eat, have been to Harley Street several times and King Edward VII's Hospital in London and I can't sing anymore… The comments I get in return are, "Oh, never mind all that, you look nice and slim," or "…weight's no good to you anyway."

↕

It's so hard for me at the moment. My friends are clearing out my caravan and it's breaking my heart. It's just another knock in the life of Chris Needs. Oh my God I wish I was straight! I've been driven out by my own people. Somehow I have to get my personal stuff out of the caravan but I don't think I can face it. My God, I loved that caravan but, over the past year, I just couldn't bring myself to spend any time there.

13 May 2013

Next Saturday Bonnie Tyler is representing the UK in the Eurovision Song Contest. I keep praying that she'll win and I'm quite sure she'll do well because she's adored by Europe. I just pray her voice will be OK and she doesn't get a cold as the weather is disgraceful, as usual.

I'm being invited to so many events at the moment and it's wonderful that people think that much of me to do so. They are really well-to-do, posh events as well, with top liners to rub shoulders with. I remember meeting HRH Princess Margaret. She was so easy to talk to. She could see that I was suffering from Bell's palsy at the time and she stroked my face with her hand and wished me well. Thought to myself, what about that then – all I need now is a trip to Benidorm and I'll be fighting fit. Lovely lady.

Time now to pop over the road to see Gabe in the shop. He's clearing out my caravan tonight with our friend Billy. I'm sat in Cwmafan; it's the middle of May and it's sleeting. What a depressing place to be. Summer in Wales. Bonnie Tyler is on my mind, big time. As long as she does her own thing and gets the sound right she'll be OK. I'll be contacting her in the next few days to wish her well. The weather is still crap and now I know that I have to leave Wales or I'll probably die of a continuing chest infection, depression or persecution for being gay. Everyone I speak to is desperate to go somewhere else. Somewhere like things used to be. The rain/sleet is so heavy at the moment I can't hear the TV.

My mother, dad and me used to go to the beach in Aberafan very often. I remember digging a hole in the sand looking for the sea because, if you dug deep enough, you'd strike water. I suppose youngsters now wouldn't know what it's like to go to a beach in this country.

I'm losing faith rapidly in this country. I've applied and paid for the deeds of some land that my mother left me but I haven't yet received them. So I've just called them and they've sent the papers to – wait for it – the plot of land. Maybe I should put some wellies on and go search in the fields for the deeds. I told the woman that it was a good job that she wasn't a surgeon – otherwise she'd be up for manslaughter. I feel like jumping off the roof!

It's quite sickening really because when I phone up businesses, they usually don't want to know and are very lackadaisical about my request – in fact, they usually don't give a toss. That is, until they realise who I am, and that I'm a voice on the radio in Wales. It's then, like by magic, they change and treat me like royalty. People are so the same aren't they. Time for insulin… ugh!

Sad, sad, sad, today. The day has come to sign away my beautiful caravan because of the daubing by an idiot. I can't keep it now as I'm afraid to go there and see the word queer back on there. So, the heavy mob has won. They've driven the queer out. I would say that normally I'm a God-fearing person, but I wonder what I'd do if I came face to face with the dickhead that daubed my caravan. A woman came into my shop the other day and said that I was a bragger… telling the world what I have. Well, if you work hard you can have what you like but, having said that, what do I have to show for it? I can't keep anything because of vandals.

I've just decided to take a week's holiday and it has to be without Gabe because of the shop and Buster needing to have one of us around for him. So, Carole Rees Jones will come with me. I'm taking a week off from the BBC which is something I never do, but I need some sun to recover from my throat and chest infections. No chance here. So I've asked the BBC for some time off – we'll see.

↕

I was going to drive to London with Gabe but I couldn't stand the bumpety-bump of the roads to be honest. So we'll go on the train – it's quick enough. Carole will be with me though, as I have treatment scheduled for my throat – only day surgery, but they'll keep me in overnight as a precaution. And, as I have to rest my voice, a trip abroad in the sunshine will work wonders. So I need to shut up for a while, but then Carole will make up for it, believe you me. I'm seeing a specialist tomorrow and I'm a bit concerned just in case one of the scars in my throat has turned nasty. You never know, to be honest. Mind you, my voice had a hammering last weekend on Eurovision night. Mal Pope and me were presenting the Eurovision show for BBC Radio Wales from the Mumbles. We were located in a little pub near where Bonnie lives and apparently frequents when she's at home. Some would say a select little venue but, to be honest, it was minuscule, overcrowded and far too noisy. It was difficult to conduct any of the interviews over the voices of visitors who had descended on the pub and had, obviously, been drinking for most of the day. We struggled to hear ourselves as the main event was relayed over the television, and I constantly strained my voice throughout the night. All I can honestly remember is that Only Boys Aloud were there and we chatted about their favourite songs in the competition, although I believe their choices were based more on the artistes' appearance and clothing or, rather, the lack of clothing! Oh, and I did an interview with a clothes designer and we talked about corsets. Say no more!

My boss has just phoned me and told me that my late show is going to be four hours instead of three. Someone must love me. My boss Steve is a lovely man, much younger than me. Mind you, most are younger than me. Steve used to be a newsreader on my afternoon show on Touch AM Radio, my old independent radio employers. But he's where he should be now and doing the job well as far as I'm concerned. It's great to have a good rapport with the boss, but it's your audience that keeps you there. I'm glad to say that the friendly Garden has changed my life and the lives of the listeners as well. It's a feeling of belonging and that's nice. My voice has been sort of OK today, thank the Lord. It's all driving me nuts.

$\updownarrow$

One of the nicest people I know is Bill. He was married to a friend of mine, Kitty from Ireland, although he is Welsh. I gave her away at their wedding and Gabe was best man for Bill. All this happened in 1994 in Ireland. I didn't think there could be a place that rained more than Wales, but Ireland holds the cup, honestly. It was a lovely trip to Ireland, but it was a bit difficult for me because my father had just died two weeks earlier and I wasn't going to go. But, my mother made me go saying that I couldn't let people down on their big day. I'm glad that I did. Sadly Kitty died and, after 16 years, Bill is now left on his own. I'm glad he still keeps in touch with us and recently moved back to south Wales. He's also helped Gabe by running errands for the shop. It's nice to have a bit of help and company.

$\updownarrow$

I've just done something I hate – I've just bitten my tongue. My tongue is pouring blood. Wow, that hurt. Anyway Delores DeLago (Louise) is due in the shop, so Gabe and me are going to town to the bank. Life is forever exciting!

$\updownarrow$

I've been to Swansea to buy some summer clothes to go to Benidorm. Sorry Swansea, but I like clothes shopping in Cardiff, London or Spain, but anywhere west of Cardiff, nothing doing! I still can't find a silk shirt. After my treatment I'm off to Spain for a short period of recuperation with not only Carole Rees Jones, but Li Harding is coming as well. Look out Benidorm. Me and Gabe can't have foreign holidays together now because of Buster; we could never leave him with someone else. I'd be crawling up the walls. So, when I come back, Gabe will take his mother, probably to Barcelona or Jersey on a shopping trip, and I'll look after the shop and Buster for a few days.

$$\updownarrow$$

I don't know what it is exactly but I'm getting frightened to go out. Years ago nothing would stop in my way but, since the incident with my caravan, I guess I'm too afraid. Who the hell said, "We'll keep a welcome in the hillside." My voice is slightly improving but the singing, no. I feel as if there's a vendetta against me and that's bloody hard to live with. I'm counting the days to Benidorm. Thank God, or Richard Branson, or whoever, for the text message service on mobile phones, otherwise I'd be out in Spain and unable to communicate with Gabe. I'm looking like mad for an apartment near the beach so that I can walk into the water every morning of my life. Carole has booked me into an all-inclusive hotel in Dénia. I mean, what more can a boy ask for? She's driving me everywhere and looking after me. Li and me have been friends for donkey's years. I love women, but men get on my tits. I bought a new jacket today and it makes me look like Quentin Crisp, but I'm more camp than he was. I'll wear it abroad, not here.

I want to organise a big concert at my chapel, Bethania, Cwmafan – the one you've seen me in on the telly. It's the one next door to the shops. I'd like to give funds raised to the hospital appeal, my charity set up in memory of my mother, and give a donation to the chapel too where my mother was a deacon. Maybe I'll ask Roy Noble and Rebecca Evans as guest speakers. I'd like that. That'll be my project for the New Year. I've got far too much going on at the moment.

I'm so worried about Gabe. He's been so unwell of late. His blood pressure had gone haywire after a change in medication and each variation has caused reactions from rashes to throat issues, severe stomach cramps, then excessive swelling of the feet, legs and thighs. It all seems to have calmed down again now that he's back on the original medication. But what appears to be arthritis in his hips, knees and ankles is much worse. He suffered a fall downstairs recently too, fracturing three ribs. I suppose we're both medical nightmares. He's the only reason I'm alive and, I have to be honest, I wouldn't know what to do if I didn't have him at my side. My only concern now is Gabe. I need to look after him more. If there was no Gabe, there'd be no me.

I'm sat on my bed and it's eight o'clock in the morning and Buster has run out of finest roast beef. Calamity! So, I'm dressing to go to Tesco as he only likes their finest range. Can you believe it? But there you go, we're all God's children. Time to go.

↕

I'm getting ready to go to Spain. I have to go as I'm running out of soap and silk shirts. I'll also be clocking the apartments to buy. I miss not having a place abroad. Gabe and me loved our place in Gibraltar and those are times we want back, and why not? Things have gone down the drain since the financial collapse but I'm determined to get back a bit of pleasure again, especially now that we've got Buster. He really is like our own child. I'm definitely buying a new plush collar for him. They do amazing dog collars in Benidorm market. There's a new stall there, Collar Mania (collarmania@yahoo.co.uk) run by ex-pats and they design and make collars with the name of your dog on them spelt in diamantés. Our dog is getting camper by the minute. Time to get holiday insurance and a few last-minute things, time for my favourite sport – shopping.

15 June 2013

I've just come back after the treatment on my throat and my trip to Spain. I don't know, but this time the visit to Spain was bloody lousy. When we landed Carole booked a car and off we went to the hotel in Benidorm. The problems started when we booked in, well, tried to book in. The booking was completely incorrect and they had booked us in nine times! Poor Carole's credit card took a hammering! It took a while, but we got it sorted. My room had an old air-conditioning unit, probably from the Boer War, which hardly worked. When it did, it was so noisy I couldn't sleep anyway.

On the second day we'd been out and about and came back to the hotel to find it in complete darkness. There was a power cut and the back-up generator wasn't working either. No lifts, no light, no food even (as they had no cooking facilities!). I needed to get to my room for my insulin shot and, traipsing up two floors practically floored me with my circulation/mobility problems. But then I couldn't get into my room, the electronic card keys didn't work as there was no power. Eventually, we were able to locate the service manager who managed to open the door with a manual override key.

There was no rest for me. The hotel installed a massive lorry outside, directly below my window, with a huge generator on it. Great, we had power restored, but the fumes were coming into my room and were quite overpowering – bear in mind that I'd just endured a throat procedure. I closed the window but the air-con was knackered at this point.

The hotel was all-inclusive, but every time I went to the bar it was closed or, if it was open, they were queuing a mile to get a drink. I ended up going next door and paying so as not to have to queue. It was all a load of crap really. One hundred degrees, no air-con, no electricity, no lifts, no drinks, no food, and Carole, poor bugger, was charged nine times. Li Harding had the right idea – she practically lived on the beach, and had a great time.

Li and me hit Benidorm market big time, and I bought some nice gear, especially for Buster. He now models for the business that makes the personalised diamanté collars! If you go to Benidorm market, which is open Wednesdays and Sundays, be sure to visit that doggie stall mentioned earlier – Collar Mania. You might even see a picture or two of Buster.

I was badly let down by the hotel this week – this week of all weeks – when I needed rest and the best of everything after the ordeal with my throat. It wasn't much recuperation – more of a survival week. It was said to me that I spoke Spanish, why didn't I complain, and I simply replied that I couldn't talk, you silly bugger. I'm supposed to be saving my voice. I was so glad to get away from there. Of course, I'll be returning, but I'll be choosing a proper posh hotel next time. No more second-hand hovels for me. No more all-inclusive no matter how many stars they've been allocated. This week has proved to be far too great an ordeal when I badly needed a break. The food was nice and that was about all. But I'll be back! *Y Viva España!*

Summer 2013

As I pass the Tower Hotel in Jersey Marine, Neath I shudder – another era in my life when I trusted people. People have been the ruination of my life. I just keep bumping into prats, and I trust them. But now I'm of the opinion that instead of everyone being lovely till they dirty on me, now it's everyone's a waster till they prove themselves to me. Sounds about right to me. No more am I going to turn the other cheek but I'll hit straight out and whack them and, if they don't like it, well tough.

↕

The island of Jersey is very much on my mind at the moment, with a reunion of people I worked with coming up in a few weeks. I had a relationship with a chap who was the manager of a few of the shows out there, and it was great because you couldn't rent anywhere there unless you had residential qualifications. I even arranged for my youngest brother to have a job there during the school holidays. In those days he was speaking to me, not that I care now one bit whether he speaks to me or not. I like the distance between us, it suits me fine. My mother used to come over whenever she could, or should I say, when she ran out of fags!

In 1982 I'd left Spain in tears to head home to Wales to take a week's break before moving to Jersey for the summer season. I was heartbroken, as I didn't really want to leave my precious Spain. There was hell in me and I was swearing at everything and everyone as I didn't want to go to Jersey. But I had signed a contract and I couldn't get out of it and that was that. The time came for me to leave Cwmafan and drive to Weymouth and board the ship in my van, full of keyboards etc. and head for the Channel Islands. My mother had prepared some food to take with me, consisting of a whole cooked chicken which I ate on the way down as if it was a bag of crisps. When it was time to board the ferry, I felt like driving into the sea but, of course, I didn't. The next thing, we were sailing over the English Channel to Jersey. The sea was so rough that even the crew were throwing up and I have to admit I've never been so seasick in my life. I was throwing up chicken everywhere. Boy, was I ill. This made me even more depressed, as Spain was calling me back and here was I heading for an island that looked like Anglesey and, boy, I didn't want to be there. I landed in St Helier and drove west to St Brelade's where my summer season Hawaiian Show was held. I met the owner of the show, Chris Savva, a Greek Cypriot and he started to shout... But, apparently, this was his way. I set up my equipment on the stage and was then taken to a bungalow and given a single room with a shared bathroom with another dozen performers. I sat in the bedroom all alone and far away from Spain wondering what the hell I was doing there. I hated it. Day by day I met the various musicians and singers under contract as they arrived from the mainland. They seemed OK, but two of the musicians seemed a bit drunk and, to be honest, I never saw them sober for the next nine months – and you know me and drink, I bloody hate it now. But we all got on...

I started my own show in the Waikiki Bar and I struck gold with the locals, the Jersey Beans as they were called. They supported me big time and the bar was packed every night, so much so that the main show next door suffered. The owner Chris asked me to do a spot in the main show there, but the bar would empty as they all left en masse to see me in that show. When I'd then return, I'd find the bar still empty but it did fill up again in a second burst and I was the flavour of the month. I was a gold mine for the owner.

Time passed and then I met Christine, my friend from Durham, and we hit it off big time. As I've mentioned already, I asked Christine if she could help me out with the problem of refilling the Waikiki Bar after the others had gone into the main show. She took holidaymakers out on island tours during the day, and so she would stop at the Hawaiian for coffee and point me out as the top Welsh entertainer, comedian and gay boy, and Bonnie Tyler's keyboard player – so the whole bus would book in for the bar that night, so I had Jersey completely sewn up. I would fill the bar, and then take them into the main show, then half-an-hour later the second lot of people, thanks to Christine, would appear.

Christine and me were really close and we planned and schemed for the future. She even came to live with me and work for me when I had the Tower Hotel in Jersey Marine. Gabe, Christine and me went back to Jersey a couple of years ago and the difference was noticeable – not a show in sight, well not like the old days, anyway. We enjoyed the trip, mind you, but she's very much like me – she prefers to live in the good old days and tries to bring them back. I've kept in contact with several people in Jersey – one of which is my friend, Trica. She recently lost her husband Steve, and they were so devoted, a really nice couple. They used to run a guest house and looked after my mam and my brother really well. I'm always looking for a cheap flight to pop over to Jersey to pay a visit.

There's one street that I like visiting on Jersey, in Saint Ouen in the north-west of the island. It's a street full of hydrangeas on both sides of the road. My mother called it Hydrangea Avenue. That brings back memories. Good times I think, very much so. On my next trip I want to see La Belle Étoile in Saint John. I'll probably be very disappointed; I reckon there'll be massive changes there, too many changes. That's the trouble with me, I live in the past constantly also. For a while I was on the TV programme, *Bergerac*, which was set in Jersey and was handy money. I saw myself on repeats recently on the telly. God, I was thin then, rather like I am now.

↕

I returned from Jersey to Wales to open the Tower Hotel. Sorriest thing I ever did. Me and my parents put all we had into the business and the guy I was with took off with a younger model and left me high and dry. Do I ever learn?

In 1986 the Tower Hotel came to an end and I had nowhere to go. I asked my mother if I could come home but the answer was no because of my siblings – my brothers. Apparently they didn't want me there and so my mother was torn.

To save her any anguish, I rented a flat in Swansea city centre, which was very nice, but I got it all wrong. I was the only one to occupy it according to the live-in landlord and landlady. They were like jailers and watched me every minute of the day to see if I had any visitors and if someone stayed over with me. One night someone did; there was uproar, and they treated me like a child. I was paying top whack for this flat, but it was managed like a hotel for idiots. I was so flabbergasted and disgusted by the way that I was treated. I told them where to go; I told her to stick her concentration camp up her boring you know where!

I bought a house in Briton Ferry. I absolutely bloody hated it there. I knew nobody and it was a big house – and I was in the wrong country, all alone wanting to go back to Spain. Spain was calling.

But before Spain and all of that, there came Neil, the hairdresser. Now here was an era. We were introduced by a mutual friend, Lorri, and we started dating. He was good for me at the beginning and helped me through some really dark times, fair play. Neither of us had any money and so I started the long, hard climb of getting back on my feet. We had a house in Barry, in fact a few doors away from where they filmed *Gavin and Stacey*. I liked Barry because it was out of the area that caused me so much heartache. I was meeting new people and I had a life, or at least the starts of one, again.

Me and Neil got on all right and so we planned to go and live abroad in Spain. I was offered a job in Benidorm singing and playing keyboards, through an agent. I packed everything, speakers, piano, all sorts! Off we went to start a new life in Spain.

But when we got to the venue, there was no job. I couldn't get hold of the agent (of course) and we were stranded out in Spain with not a lot of money, nowhere to stay and no job. I was bloody evil and, if I'd seen that agent, I'd have swung for him. But me being me, I managed to find a few nights' work entertaining in a place down the road, thank goodness, and I earned enough for us to have a small apartment and enough to eat. Eventually, the other place where I was supposed to work offered me a job there. So I had two jobs and boy, was I doing well. The next thing, the agent contacted me and asked for commission for the work that I was doing. Can you I imagine what my reaction was? I exploded and used a few Russian words all ending with —off!

That's so typical of some people. They want everything and they're not prepared to do anything for it. Needless to say I never worked for that idiot of an agent ever again. Even today I find that some people must have gone to college to study how to become an idiot!

I stayed in Spain for years and loved it. I came home eventually and, looking back, it was the worst move I've ever made in my life. The ridicule was massive from some people and I cried myself to sleep once again. Why did I come back? Probably for the sake of my parents. Silly me. I remember sitting in a lousy workmen's club, the rain pouring outside, with bingo on in the main hall, and I sat in the gents' toilet wanting to slit my wrists. What the hell was I doing here? I'd made a big mistake.

In saying that, I'm still in Wales – at the moment, and still putting up with hassle after hassle. I have to say it's really hard when people have a stab at you and ridicule you for being gay. It wouldn't happen in London and certainly not on the continent. I now feel, at the age of 59, that I've wasted my life and I can't go back and start again, unfortunately.

If I had my life to live over again I'd try to have a more normal life – a job in the bank. Boy, they've had it made haven't they? And maybe try and be *straight* so that I wouldn't be the victim of hate attacks and violence. If I had a child maybe none of this crap would've taken place. But this is where I am in life and I've got to make the best of it. I'm not prepared to put up with abuse any longer. So I'd be very careful if you fancy a pop at me, because don't forget, I'm training to be another J.R. Ewing. So there!

Chapter 12

MY NEW AGENT wants me to go to London for an audition. I think it could very well be for an advert. He won't tell me, he said it's a surprise. I hope it's not an audition to be a stripper! Pity the audience! They'd be put off men forever!

I'm sure I have this condition called obsessive compulsive disorder (OCD). I'm getting upset all of the time because I can't find a V-neck T-shirt anywhere. Well, not the type I want. I know where they sell them in Berlin and in Spain, so I could buy a few of them there, but what would I arrive in? Am I sad?

Good news: Carole Rees Jones is coming to see me on Thursday – she'll sort me out! She knows just about everything. She'll sort out a V-neck for me.

I keep looking to see if there are any nice cheap deals to visit Spain, Jersey or Berlin. I'm long overdue a visit. I'm overdue visiting anywhere abroad!

It's very hard living in Cwmafan compared to Cardiff. There's so much in Cardiff, and boy do I miss it. There's a place in Cwmafan called The Gorad. Lots of youngsters go there to swim. I asked where it was and was told about a mile up the road from my shops. I thought it was a Leisure Centre but it turns out to be a bridge and a deep part of the river, and the kids jump off the bridge into the water. That's the nearest to a Leisure Centre we'll get here in the land of the moving curtains.

When in Cardiff I miss the greetings from people around me in Cwmafan such as, "Where are you going to?" or "Slumming it here are you?" Friendly bunch! Fortunately not all of them!

And there are so many shops in Cardiff. I tried to do some clothes shopping in Port Talbot – fatal; there are so few shops of any description these days. Sad. I used to love popping into Cole's for jeans in Aberafan, oh, and not forgetting the old Cloth Hall.

Buster knows I'm all uptight and he's *cwtching* me every minute that he can. He's such a good boy. I'm preparing for his birthday party. He has a 'do' every year and this year he'll be three years old. While I'm out, I'll be looking for a present for him. His favourite is a dolly. Any stuffed toy with eyes and limbs is a dolly! He loves his toys and his dollies!

I actually went out to buy more underpants – not that I needed them – but they were designer, brightly coloured and on offer! But, I'm cracking up at the moment, looking for clothes that look good on me. I'm not about to make the mistake of trying to look young or as mutton dressed up as lamb. I'm trying to look good for my age. I must be doing something right as everybody tells me that I don't look nearly 60. I don't try creams and lotions; I firmly believe that music and being on stage keeps me young. After all I've been through with my health, I really should have died.

23 July 2013

I'm appearing on Chris Corcoran's programme called *Come the Revolution* tomorrow. It's going to be a bit of a hit or miss. People love gay on stage or on air, but they don't like it in real life. Try living with that situation – it must be OK because it's on the BBC. But the minute I step off-stage, it's different. That's a hard thing to cope with. You're OK if you're a product, but nothing else. I have to be honest I'm bloody fed up of being the court jester. I want to do something more serious. I'd like to appear on *Value Judgements*. I loved being on Max Boyce's programme, *The Final Curtain*. It was a chat show where Max would ask his guests as to where they'd like to spend their last day, their last meal and who with, and it was a really good programme. I wanted to spend my last days in Gibraltar with a paella and Margaret Thatcher, wearing a thong (me, not Mrs T) and being tanned and a bit taller. I'd want all the boys to wolf whistle at me as I strolled along the beach. That's what I call a dream! I had a dream once that I was in Wales and it *never* rained for 40 days and 40 nights – I'll never forget that *dry* dream. He-he-he! (sorry).

↕

So, last night I appeared on the Chris Corcoran show at the BBC Club in Cardiff. It seemed that it was going to be hard work for me but I couldn't have been more wrong. Chris let me run wild! The gay aspect of things worked a treat. The audience was eating out of my hand. I sang 'I am what I am' and the audience sobbed. Mind you, I'm not sure if it was the song or my ropey voice of late. I thought that I wouldn't fit in, as most comedians today have gone modern/alternative but I'm still like the old school, i.e. Bernard Manning etc.

I like a good yarn and seeing people having a belly laugh. My God, we don't laugh enough today.

Just had the call from Carole Rees Jones; I'm being taken to lunch in Swansea. She drives all the way from Aberystwyth as if she's just popping down the shops for a pint of milk. I could never do it; three hours to anywhere from there. I'd be dead in a week. She drives to Spain as if she's just going for a run somewhere. The strength of that woman is quite incredible. I wish I had half her strength, believe you me – and she takes her dogs everywhere with her. I can't even look after myself.

I'm planning a new opening for the charity shop at 5 Bethania Terrace, the shop next door to Gabe's in Cwmafan. It's been a long time coming but, what with being so ill over the last few years, a lot of things have been put on hold. People ask me "Why bother?" and I tell them the same thing always – if I didn't, I'd die. I have to be doing something or other – anything, a bingo caller in Benidorm – just as long as I'm in there seeing to something. I think that if I just sat in the house doing nothing with a shawl over my legs, I'd simply die. So the charity shop is next on the agenda. A lot of stuff to get rid of, such as videos which are quite obsolete right now. It's been fun with the shops because it's a place that listeners can just pop into and, believe me, there've been a few. I'll never forget the opening back in 2001. There were celebrities galore and even a brass band playing out in the street. Local people brought chairs out onto the pavement and sat there in their ringside seat enjoying all the nonsense that was going on. The first person in the shop was Brian Hibbard from The Flying Pickets. He came in dressed in his trademark leopard skin jacket, with a quarter of boiled sweets. Then he took his teeth out and smiled for the photographers! What a dude. So there are many memories attached to the shops and, for the moment, they'll probably be the last thing to go.

Ideally, in my own crazy little world, I'd like a shop that just sold V-neck T-shirts. Like I've already said, I'm nuts about V-neck T-shirts. Don't ask me why.

So, I'm looking forward to getting stuck into the new venture, although I've had many people ask could they buy both shops. So, in a way, I've covered myself as there's always someone looking for a business opportunity.

I love the weekends and, by Thursday, I start getting urges to book a weekend away to somewhere like Jersey, Spain or Andorra. I could quite easily go away every weekend, which leads to the question, why don't I just bugger off anyway? The main reason stopping me is my BBC programme. I feel that if the Garden show went, a lot of people would feel it bad. They'd be lonely and deserted. It's never been just a radio programme; it's always been a community centre and a community centre for real. I'm sure people realise how important the company the programme gives is. I'm often told, to my face, how much the programme is needed. And yes, there's also the job aspect for me and a wage and a chance to go out and perform on stage, which I adore. But I know the glorious day will come and I'll know when the time is right. It's strange isn't it? I've worked my guts out all my life to own a home here and I've longed for the day when I'd paid everything off and could sit back a bit, *but* after all that hard work and name-calling etc., I finally realise that I don't want to be here and, to be honest, I've never wanted to be here. I need to go home to Spain. And so the glorious day gets nearer and nearer. I have to go. One cannot live in total unhappiness.

When I appeared on Chris Corcoran's show recently, one of the questions asked was "Where is your favourite place? Wales or England?" Before I could answer, the whole audience shouted together, "Spain". They all know me. I'm an oddity and I've never met anyone quite like me. I'm not saying I'm cool or right, but I'm certainly different. And I'm sorry that I am in a lot of ways. I sometimes envy people that have never been anywhere or done anything. I think now, looking back, I believe I could cope with normality. It would be a nice change. Also, being 'public property' doesn't appeal to me, it never has. I tell everyone that I'm not paid enough to be owned by anyone. Life is getting harder as I get older. The more famous I get, the more I'm pestered by so many people, here *and* abroad and even in my own property. Fortunately, not everyone I meet wants to pester me. There are the nice people who just want to stop and chat for a while, to let me know what's been troubling them and tell me that they get so much out of my radio show and how it's helped them. It makes me feel good that they've found ways of helping themselves while listening to others on the show with similar problems.

↕

Well, I'm sat in the middle of a heatwave *here in Wales*... and all I seem to hear is "Oh, it's too hot" and "I can't stick this heat." In a few weeks they pop back into the shop saying they were in Cyprus last week and it was 45 degrees and it was wonderful, which makes me think that maybe it's wrong to have good times here. God only knows, I'd love some good times. I've had enough crap flung at me. I feel very used in just about every aspect of my life lately and I don't like it. Please God give me a happy life. My mother went out an unhappy woman and I'll definitely do the same. I'm becoming a bit of a handful for my friends as they must be fed up of hearing the same old thing over and over, such as, "Why doesn't Wales like me?" and "Why does it rain so much?" and the list goes on. When I need cheering up I go on the computer, onto YouTube and look at places in Spain. I love that, I really do. Places mean so much to me. I remember when my mother died I sat and watched the film *Escape from East Berlin* hundreds and hundreds of times. Gabe must have been demented as a result.

I'm about to start my day job, the usual cooking, shopping, paying bills etc. and, as always, hoping something nice will happen to me instead of all the crap that I get – and something has! I've been asked to go to an event to raise money for a guide dog association and I'll be taken for a walk blindfolded and rely completely on a guide dog. I can't wait.

My voice is certainly much, much stronger but still 'up and down'. I'm now having therapy every week which seems to be helping. Just talking to the therapist is a great comfort.

$$\updownarrow$$

It's Tuesday. I wake up this morning deflated to hell and back. Monday nights are important; after a weekend I need to have a good show on a Monday to set a precedent for the week, but I never got the chance last night. The whole computer system playing the songs broke down – again. This is becoming a regular occurrence and so, after a night of apologizing and pulling my hair out, how can I have a good day today? What will pull me back up?

$$\updownarrow$$

The Gwyn Hall in Neath burnt down a while back and I can't wait to see it again when it's rebuilt. I know that nothing is for ever, but I'm thrilled that The Gwyn Hall will be back. The same happened to the Afan Lido. I've yet to hear how that one's coming along. I hope it'll all come back, but I can't imagine it'll be anything like the original. My life was better in previous years, too. It would be nice to see a few things come back like they used to be in the good old days.

↕

Oh! I've just heard Susanna say on *BBC Breakfast* that the hot weather is on its way back. Not such a bad day after all. Yippee. Back I go online, looking at flights to Spain so I can dream and fantasize.

Chapter 13

WHERE WAS I? The worst is yet to come. Let me tell you about my Sunday (yesterday). I had to get my VAT accounts in sharp again to my accountant as I'd forgotten what the date was and I'd normally have it done by now. So there I am, seven o'clock Sunday morning, sat in the dining room going through hundreds and hundreds of receipts. What a way to start the day. Not even the VAT man works on a Sunday morning. Anyway, I manage to get it all done by ten. I make Gabe two bacon rolls with brown sauce and take it up to him in bed. I have a shower and I'm chuffed.

Gabe gets up and goes in the shower and I go downstairs and, after a little while, the water is pouring through the ceiling like hell. I scream to Gabe, "Get out of the shower!" and I start mopping up the mess. We then make our way to Cardiff with Buster to drop off my VAT to my accountant. Afterwards we make our way to Gabe's mam's house. Always a massive welcome whenever we turn up. She opens the door with a bowl of cold water for Buster – well, he's the important one, and we sit down to have tea and sandwiches and Welsh cakes. We then make our way to the Bay to Demiro's Restaurant, which is almost opposite the Millennium Centre. The reason for this is because Carole Rees Jones is singing there, called in to do a last-minute show. So, to show support, we pop there for half an hour as she performs outside in the sun and that means we can take Buster with us and sit outside. The Bachelors are there as well, so I finally meet the Irish boys. (I'd already interviewed them previously over the telephone.)

Then we call in at the Cash & Carry to get cigarettes and

some sweets etc. for the shop. So I watch Buster outside and give him water in his bowl and then he cries and cries – for Gabe, as usual! Anyway, out comes Gabe with a trolley full of goods for the shop – not just the cigarettes! We load up and off we go back to the land of the moving curtains. We spend ages unloading and then pricing the goods and eventually we finish. So we go over to the house and we have a bit of kip. Well deserved, trust me. I then prepare a lovely meal: Pembrokeshire new potatoes, salad etc. Then I notice a couple of Kung-fu films with Jackie Chan in them are on TV, so that's me made up.

As we sit there in the front room, we hear an almighty crash from the kitchen and when we look, the ceiling has come down on top of just about everything. I immediately think, where's Buster? But, I'm glad to say that he's lolling on the chesterfield in the front room or, as my mother would say, the parlour. The whole ceiling came down and it went in every place imaginable. Dishes were broken, saucepans knackered, the carpet was a mess and the smell was gross. Gabe was up all night cleaning the mess. I left him in bed in the morning, and called the insurers. What hard work the questions were! But thank goodness for them; otherwise, with my luck and the disasters I incur, I'd be bankrupt with everything. So today, Monday, I'm waiting for someone to check for asbestos, and a surveyor, a plumber, a plasterer and an insurance man... and a carpet cleaner. I've had a bloody guts-full. Why me?

What else will go wrong I wonder? Nothing, I hope.

I was talking to my manager Spencer and I told him that I wanted something nice to happen, as lately there's only been hassle. I've had another death threat, by the way. Why are people here so nasty to me? They've got short memories. I've done my best to raise money for all sorts, especially hospitals, the ones they probably use. I don't know why I bother. In fact, I'm winding down. I think we'll sell my property off. I think you know what's coming! I'm thinking right now of a Queen song, 'I want to break free'! Watch me!

This insurance claim is going to be a right pig's ear. I've

stayed in and nobody has come – sounds so British, doesn't it! Next thing, here we go, a plumber turns up – nine hours late – strolls in, looks at it and says we don't cover you for this and off he goes. So today is another battle to get something sorted.

Just had the asbestos man in to check the house for any traces of the dangerous stuff. Three days for a result. He could have tested my diabetes while he was at it.

The surveyor has just been, at nine o'clock. They know I work nights! He's examined the damage, took photos galore and all *is* covered and *will* be put right, asap. Thank goodness. Any more problems and I think I'll jump off a cliff!

↕

The piano might be coming back to my radio programme and I think it'll do well. Many years ago I used this feature on Radio Cymru, so it's tried and tested. What I have to do is play a request for someone but, here's the point – I play it out of tune like Les Dawson used to. That'll be different; no other radio station does this as far as I'm aware.

The weather is back to Welsh normal rubbish. But they do say that the hot weather is coming back with a vengeance. Bring it on, that's what I say. Let me frazzle baby, let me frazzle! But I'm still on the moving trip and Spain is crying out for me to go there. I can't let it cry for me, I'll have to go and look after the country! Gabe has just given me the front headline of the newspaper: "Heatwave to return, 95 degrees." Is that all? Mean buggers.

↕

I'm pleased for Gabe as his shop is picking up nicely and he's more relaxed about things. It's always hard opening a new business, especially in these times when people haven't got much money. When I'm sat in the shop, I'm taken back to the days when my mother ran it. And lots more of memories come flooding back again – like the time when a lady came in and asked for fig rolls, toilet rolls, Swiss rolls, and a quarter of Riley's toffee rolls. Then there was the time when an old lady asked my mother for a sachet of shampoo but my mother gave her the wrong sachet. She gave her a sachet of conditioner. The old dame came back the next day saying that she wasn't fussed on that shampoo she was given as there was not a lot of lather. My mother said it must have been for greasy hair. Another time, my mother would be stood ready to serve her customers and a woman came in and said that she'd been cold all morning, and my mother agreed with her saying that she'd been cold all morning, too. Next thing, another woman came in and said that she was really warm. My mother again agreed with her, saying that she'd been sweating conkers all morning, too. No wonder my mother died a rich woman. Very rich indeed.

Chapter 14

August 2013

Sunday is a special day. I think Sundays were made for radio. The wireless sounds better on a Sunday by a mile. The 'Best Bits' was a compilation of highlights from my evening shows during the week. Listeners were upset and moaned when it went from a Saturday to a Sunday. I think there'll be a few disappointed people about now that the 'Best Bits' have gone altogether. I believe the British are a nation of no change. We don't like change and neither do I. I'm now wondering how I'm going to cope with the increase to a four-hour show nightly in the new schedule. My day at home will be shorter, another change! We'll see. There are some new features planned for the show; in addition to the piano, there'll be unsung heroes, the songs of your life, G&T around midnight, the Latin quarter – well, lots and lots of Spanish. What do you expect? And we'll be inviting people to sing on air and become a star for the evening. All good, I think. I just hope I don't peg out during it all. And *I* must remember it's a nine o'clock start.

More tales of my mother

My mother had a code when she was hungry and boy, could my mother eat. She'd start coughing quietly and making funny noises with her lips; she looked like a goldfish. And for a simple life, I'd drive up to Miss Millie's and buy her some southern fried chicken. I'd phone her from the takeaway and ask her what she wanted, e.g. two pieces and one chips or three pieces and two chips or maybe a bargain box with coleslaw and trimmings or, finally, what about a family bucket of chicken and six chips and beans and coleslaw and pop etc.? She'd say get the family bucket. When I'd get back, I'd walk in with the family bucket and my mother would say, "Where's yours then?" Bloody typical and very true!

↕

I'm sat up in bed as I can't sleep because of the pain in my legs, i.e. the old diabetes playing up again. And once again I'm wondering what will this week bring?

I get bad vibes on a Sunday night just like I did when I had to go to Dyffryn Comprehensive School on a Monday back in the bad old days. Do you know there's never been a time when I haven't stuck my middle finger up to that school as I'm passing on the motorway! Then, about half a mile further on, I pass where my mother is buried, which is on the right, and I turn my head to the left not to see the place, as if to convince myself that it's not there. Life is getting stranger for me by the minute.

I've just completed a written piece for a book entitled *It's OK to be Gay*. Well-known figures in the gay community were asked to share their experiences of coming to terms with their sexuality and 'coming out' to their family and friends. The account was very true, but it was the end bit that got me. I made myself and the producers on my show, Sian Evans and Llinos Jones, cry when reading it. I said something along the lines that today it's much easier for gay people; they, at long last, have rights, but when I was young I had no rights. I was just a punch bag/clown back then. The piece went on to say that the happiest day of my life was when I got wed to Gabe. And people say it's OK now to do all this, but a bit bloody late for me. I'm told that people can be prosecuted for ridiculing me, just like racists' comments, and yet I can't help feeling disgusted at what I am sometimes, because it was driven into me all of my life that simply to be gay was mega wrong. I

121

still feel this now. I try and get over this by being as 'open' as possible on the radio.

Life is so strange here. I want out asap.

Well Monday has arrived and, guess what, it's hammering down, so bad that there's flooding out in the street. I got soaked yesterday and I seem to have a sore throat – just what the doctor ordered after what I've had done to my throat – not that I trust many after my ordeal. I'm trying to fathom out how weather presenters can be so happy when they give us the latest forecast. They smile when there's flooding and seem happy whenever the weather is bad. How can they do that? It's their job! Oh, how I wish it would stop raining.

It's a week away from the new show on the radio and I'm truly concerned about the whole lot of it. Radio is my world and I'll never allow anything or anyone to mess with it, whoever they are. Once I let go of the reigns, I've had it. I've got to keep my stamp on it.

You can't beat a bit of fuss. I remember once a lady working in Newport, Gwent, won a box of chocolates for being a good neighbour. On this occasion, it was an extremely hot day and by the time I'd travelled to her place of work, with the chocolates in the car as well, I walked in and practically poured them onto the counter! The weather is always wrong here in Wales.

So far today I've only had 22 of the usual "How are yous?" and I say the same thing to them all, "Terrible, thanks," and I get the same answer back "Oh, very good."

I'm terrible at packing and I'm working hard for this weekend I'm spending in Jersey. I'm taking my iPad because I've sensibly booked the Hotel de France which has free Wi-Fi there. The trouble is, with being self-employed, if you miss a phone call from a booker you've usually lost the gig. So the iPad and iPhone go with me.

↕

The amount of letters I receive from gay people is quite

astonishing. I'm told the same thing over and over; you give us a voice. It's good that gay people in Wales have a place to go to at night, a gay-friendly place. It's so important. A young gay boy wrote to me in confidence and asked me did I think he could have contracted Aids? But this is what I mean; gay is still taboo in many parts of Wales. Even I feel dirty when some people meet me and the looks they give me. So I put this young lad right. So to me, the programme is so very important in many ways. It's there as a public service.

I mainly play the songs requested; after all, I'm entertaining you, I'm not entertaining me. But having said that, I do like the choice of music. It's crazy, like me. People from other radio stations ask me about the music policy on my programme and I tell them anything goes! They are all envious of the show as they'd love to play the wide choice that I play but they can't because they are governed by the pop charts, whereas me and Radio Wales are not.

I've just found out that an old friend of mine is the editor of BBC Radio Jersey. Unfortunately, when I'm over this weekend, he's away on holiday. I must catch up with him. You never know... I do love Jersey. If they're looking for an old queer presenter, I'm your boy.

$$\updownarrow$$

We drive home through Port Talbot every night after the show and generally the smell is bearable although, some nights, when the works release the sulphur, or whatever it is, it stinks to high heaven. Maybe that's why we pay such high rates here. We must be paying for the smell. My God, I was nearly sick. Now if I'd opened a business and that smell came from my premises, I'd probably be done for it, I suppose.

Never mind, *Dallas* is on at seven. Can't watch it live any more because of the new times of my programme. I have to record it so as not to miss it. What I do in the name of entertainment! Me putting J.R. on hold!

Carole Rees Jones called me this evening and she could hardly talk. She was devastated, crying like a baby. Her little dog, Daisy May, had been run over and died. I couldn't cope with that.

I remember my mother, just after my father died, looking at TV in the night. She couldn't sleep and TV was the answer. I had a different satellite system because I like Dutch and Spanish programmes. I asked my mother one day what was she was watching overnight. The naughty girl was watching blue movies with characters such as Samantha and her wandering snake, Harry Hard On and Betty Blower. Then she went on to say that there was a nude woman singing and she was a well-endowed girl and instead of singing memories, she was singing mammories! One wild woman, but grief stricken too...

Chapter 15

WELL, WHAT A disaster. I get to the airport in Cardiff because I'm on my way to Jersey, get through security after virtually stripping, and I sit down in the first seat in the lounge waiting to board the plane. I'm very therapeutically watching the suitcases been plonked on the conveyor belt going up from the ground and into the plane's hold. I recognise my case and the guy just plonked it on, on its side and, as it travelled up the conveyor belt, it started to wobble. Other travellers were now watching and started to point. Then, as it got to the top, it fell off. People started laughing (how typically British) and my case came crashing down to the ground. I'm in a state of shock. The first thing that comes to me is thoughts about my insulin because I'm told not to carry liquids or sharp instruments in my hand luggage. I go mental; there are people laughing, so I tell them to shut up and I go to the senior-looking chap. I want the culprit's name but he won't give it to me. Then I say that I need my case checked before we take off, otherwise I have no insulin and that could be fatal. The guy says that if I check the case, the plane would lose its take-off slot. So, me being me, I say I'll check it when I arrive in Jersey. Stupid me, looking after the people that were just laughing at my misfortune! I wish I'd checked it now. I opened the case in Jersey and the insulin containers had smashed. I took it to the representative and she couldn't stick the smell. She managed to fill in the forms. Due to the damage, I had no clothes to wear and no insulin to live! I'll have to start becoming inconsiderate and become a right swine.

I sat there in Jersey feeling awful on that Sunday as there

was nothing open. I didn't know of a local doctor and I was so weak I couldn't get out of bed. Thank you baggage handlers Cardiff. I couldn't get the culprit's name but I'll never forget what he looked like. Someone is going to pay for this. Trust me. A new day is dawning for the new me. I have to change as nobody cares a damn.

It's the first time that I've felt the need for Twitter or Facebook. I tried to get some insulin by social media, but the insulin apparently that I'm on is not common. However, social media did give me some hope, and that's a first.

I wish I'd never gone to Jersey. Looking back, I could've died and all because of one stupid man at the airport – and he's still throwing bags here, there and everywhere, I guess.

There's so many stupid things about today; we seem to have lost the plot. Another is how everything is managed by computers. I keep having letters from the bank about an overdraft that was paid off ages ago. I speak to people at the bank and all I get is, it's the computer – but that's not good enough.

It's August – time for overcoats and umbrellas and central heating. Oh, how I wish I lived in the sun and not here. It's so depressing. Never mind, I've got speech therapy today.

My appointment was to start at 1.30 p.m. but, as the therapist opened her door to call me in, a woman, apparently her boss, i.e. management, barged into the room to talk business with the therapist. Now to me that manager put herself before the patient. Bloody typical. She was in there for nearly half an hour. When she eventually came out, I said that she ought to be ashamed of herself and that I felt a four-letter word coming on – which was BUPA. Never again will I go to the NHS. It's back to Harley Street for me. That's that!

↕

Back to my ceiling, the one that fell into the kitchen because the shower was leaking. The insurance have taken three weeks to sort it out and, lo and behold, after three weeks of plumbers and builders etc. it still leaks. No shower, bugger all. Just my luck. My friend said to me, "Chris if you had Aids they'd cure you and then the following day you'd be run over by a bus." So will I ever shower again?

I've started the new four-hour show now and it's very busy since I've brought back the Daisy chain and a few old features. I'm really happy with it all so far.

Roy Noble called me last night as I was on my way to the studio. We had a good old chat as we always do. I miss him in the mornings, and another thing I miss is the Elimination quiz with Sian Evans. That was so good. I think we need something like Radio 2's got Pop Master. We should have a quiz in the mornings. That would be awesome.

I'm so pleased too us Welshies are on national TV: Siân Lloyd on *BBC Breakfast* and Frances Donovan doing the sport on the same programme.

Another Sunday, the weekends come around so fast. I wanted to go to Cardiff but we ended up in Swansea. We drove past the house that my old friends from the band Aquarius, Barry and Aileen Haynes, lived in, in Carmarthen Road. The great times I spent in that house, it was just incredible. I always remember trying to pull out onto the main road and the traffic was so busy that I was there for about five minutes. So Barry used to walk across the nearby zebra crossing. I just sat there wondering why he did that. I just didn't realize at the time that he'd done it so I could pull out. Back in those days, in the 1970s, I was a bit naive. In the fleeting moment when we passed the house, so many happy memories returned. Unfortunately, time just moves on too, and the only member of the band still alive, other than me, is Reg, the bass player. I need to call and see him, not just chat on the phone. I can't believe it's 40 years since we met up. Frightening.

↕

On the news today they're saying that house prices are on the up. That will give people hope. It has for me. My friend in Jersey has just sold her house for £400,000 but it was valued at £700,000 before the crash. It's one crazy world. My mother used to say "Live for today and you'll live forever." I look back at the 1970s and think to myself, "Come back, all is forgiven." I'm sick of people saying to me, it's OK for people like me. What do they mean – people like me? Do I get a *gay* pension or something? Anything I've got I've worked for and I planned and prayed to get on in show business and it's still hard. But some are of the opinion that, because I'm well known and on the radio and TV, I'm indestructible. You must be joking. I pay for everything going. I don't get anything for nothing. I pay through the nose.

↕

I feel as if there's something brewing – something that might possibly change my life. My throat is very slowly getting better, but it's still a worry and always on my mind. I keep getting thoughts about my past and the things that I've had to deal with all of my life and I'm getting flashes from my mother which always disturbs me because she tries to tell me something in a certain way. It sounds crazy but there's definitely something in the air. I'm sat in bed sobbing my heart out. I know what it's like to be a child and frightened, as I was brutally attacked as a child. And I'm looking at what's happening in Syria and the chemicals and the suffering and death of those poor children. Then there's an advert that has just been on TV – cruelty to babies. Where the hell are we living? How did we get to this state? I think of a newborn baby and I wonder which day will it turn into a terrorist? What happens to turn a person into a monster? Is it money or power or jealousy? Oh how I wish I had a magic wand. As I've said, I'd love to be in power in government. I wouldn't be fannying about; I'd be so direct I'd probably get shot or something.

↕

One of the features on my programme is the Songs of Your Life and last night I read out a letter from a guy in Ireland. It was so sad and the songs chosen were so special to the couple – two men who were an item but one had recently died. The lyrics were so moving I fell apart on air and cried and so did Llinos. I'm such a stupid cow at times. We both are – me and Llinos.

Just got to bed at about 2.15 a.m. in Cwmafan and I've just started writing again and I'm weeping again. I'm so worried about my dear friend Teddi Munro. She's now in Velindre Hospital in Cardiff. I adore Teddi and we've been friends for donkey's years. I just hope that when I see her tomorrow she'll be looking better and be able to carry on. I'm going to pray for her tonight. I will answer to The Lord as I've answered to my Lord all my life. I just hope He'll be good to Teddi.

I'm frightened to put the news on as I don't want to see any more people, especially those children in the Middle East, being chemically poisoned. I can't take it tonight. I'll have one of those rare nights when the telly stays off. I'm considering cutting right back on doing stage shows around the place for a number of reasons – mainly because of too much strain on my throat and the worry of will I sell enough tickets. Times are hard. However much people want to see me, if they're faced with the choice of paying the electric bill or coming to see Chris Needs, the bill always wins, and I understand. But people do love to go out to a Garden bash; they get to meet each other in the Garden and that's priceless and it's an excuse to make new friends. Nothing wrong with that in my book. The Garden seems to be having a new lease of life. It's getting bigger and better. Thank The Lord. I need to do another *Songs of Praise* type of programme, too. I feel safe when I work with God. That's true as well. There's a something or someone wrapping themselves around me in church or when I'm playing a nice old hymn on the piano or organ. I feel safe. Thank goodness. I'm going to try and sleep but I don't think I will. Too much on my mind.

$\updownarrow$

Off today to see Teddi. I hope I like what I see. Then off to see my manager, Spencer. He's got a lot to sort out for me. So many legal things, letters to write etc. Nothing that can't be sorted out but letter writing is a task I don't like.

$\updownarrow$

It's Sunday and it's the only day that me and Gabe have to go anywhere. But of course today, as luck would have it, we have to stay in and look after the bloody shop as it's having new electrics put in. So here I am stuck in Cwmafan. People say "Don't you like it here in Cwmafan?" and I have to be truthful, there's very little here for me. And you definitely couldn't compare it to Cardiff. There's everything in Cardiff: shops, ice rink, theatres and privacy. Lovely.

I started a rumour, just for a laugh, that I was turning one of my shops into a sex shop. Most were disgusted; mind you one or two were interested. There you go. Life takes some strange twists and turns!

People never cease to amaze me and most of them think that I'm still that vulnerable little boy. They speak to me as if I've just landed a job in my mother's shop. They don't realise that I speak to thousands of people and have a good job at the BBC. I've lived a long time and I firmly believe that I'm only alive because of my wisdom. I listen to me, not someone who thinks they know all. I think because I've done well and I'm well known, some people have to try and match me. They always seem to make out that they're bigger and better than they are. I'm not interested what people do because, without my listeners, I'm nothing. So there's no real need to impress by adding things like manager or qualified etc. I'm not that type of person. Just get on with your life and enjoy it. Oh, and keep listening to me on the radio.

↕

Life seems to be a war zone as soon as I step out of the house. I'm convinced that 90 per cent of it is jealousy. I earn well and I have a lifestyle to die for really, but then I work hard as well. But people forget that I've never abused my position and I've always given to good causes. I have to say that I'm nearly 60 and I'm disliking more people virtually by the minute. There are a few that are lovely and that's it, I'm afraid.

Also, I find the standard of workmanship is practically non-existent. Like I've said, I've had workmen here for five weeks and I still can't use the upstairs shower.

It's a week away from my concert at Porthcawl's Grand Pavilion and I have to put the show in order. Gabe's so good at sorting, after all he's been pen-pushing for years and between being involved with me and the music, I'd be best to let him sort it all out.

Been to see Teddi again today and she looks much better. Her partner Sue was there, too. She wanted to get online with her little computer but there was no Wi-Fi connection, so I lent her my Wi-Fi box and a portable Wi-Fi signal, so she's all connected up now and not so bored. At least we can email each other. I'm well pleased with that and so is she.

Chapter 16

31 August 2013

I'm stood once again on the stage at Porthcawl Grand Pavilion. The room is as full as it could be. The atmosphere is electric and I'm looking out at the audience and it seems to be like the old days. There are old friends, new friends and, most importantly, original Garden members and the feeling is good. Now I'm thinking, will my voice hold out? But it's OK, it does, and the audience seem to really like what I'm doing.

There was a very moving moment when young Jack showed us his Olympic torch. Jack was disabled in a car accident. His grandmother, Maureen, turned to the Garden for support and a lot of prayers were said by a lot of members. Jack is a survivor; it took time, but he's come on in leaps and bounds now. Although doing well, Jack has been left visually impaired. He's continued with his college studies and is looking to teach Braille and the other skills which he is mastering. He was chosen to be a part of the Olympic torch relay team through Bridgend last year.

I felt so honoured as he handed the torch to me, and something clicked in the room. This lad was a dedicated sportsman and a talented rugby player and, in spite of life-changing events, he remains positive. The people were so moved by his inspiration and, as I held the torch high in the air, the mood went crazy.

The show was one of the best ever. Peter Karre, our Welsh 'Phantom of the Opera' was sensational; Ceri Dupree was a breath of fresh air impersonating many of our favourite female celebrities; Carole Rees Jones and Bruce Anderson, fresh from their various tours were wonderful, as were the June Bois Dancers. The evening was special for Tammi Bois though, as she came away from the dance troupe to sing a duet with me in the spotlight in addition to a solo number. She did so well and already has a following as part of my team back on the radio. She must do more.

Buster, however, stole the show – again! He saunters out, looks at the audience the whole time, jumps up to kiss me and then rushes off. He loves the limelight – and being spoiled rotten!

I couldn't have planned the show any better. But the one person that held it all together was Gabe. He sorted the music out, made certain the correct backing tracks were played, liaised with the theatre staff and, more importantly, he sorted the artistes out as well. Teddi usually stage managed the show and her presence was greatly missed. It was 'well done' to Gabe, as he also had to make decisions front of house while working from the sound booth and relaying instructions backstage.

My next show is at the Riverfront Theatre in Newport and I know that'll be a really good evening as Dame Mandy Starr will be there, and also Rob Allen, the country singer.

I don't know what I would do if I couldn't walk on a stage again and perform. I've said it before – I'd probably die. Even a doctor has said to me that he doesn't know how I survived my illness. People were lighting candles for me. People ask me the same question all of the time: "You lost seven stone in eight months?" and I tell them, "No, I lost seven stone in eight *weeks*!" I still can't get my head around that. If I've survived this far after all that, I reckon I'll never die!

I've just had a funny thought. My mother years ago asked me to help her do a clear out in the house. I started in the cupboard under the stairs. So I started throwing out silly things like plastic bags and old newspapers etc. Then I discovered the pièce de résistance; I found a pack of sanitary towels (unused) and I asked my mother did she need these and she said: "I haven't used them for 20 years – give them to charity." As if!

I have to visit London soon to be checked over again, which means I'll be there overnight, but I don't want to lose a night's show, so I'm hoping to do my show from BBC London. It should be interesting seeing the big boys at work. I might even get to meet up with Janice Long again.

I'll be glad when I'm completely better. It's not been fun at all. I just want my life back. I try to keep away from people during the day because it means I have to talk to them and I'm still not supposed to speak then, so as not to strain my voice. A very difficult situation. If I don't speak to someone they say, "What an ignorant git," but if I speak I start getting hoarse and then they ask why I'm bothering to speak. I just can't win. So, whenever possible, I hide in the day.

I was playing a song the other night on the radio and there were scratches on the CD. They now put scratches on music as it's supposed to be trendy. When we were young we wouldn't touch the record in case we scratched it. How times have changed. It's even trendy to be gay these days. I'll never get my head around it.

I had words the other day with a terrorist (i.e. a receptionist). To be honest I'm not sure what she was! But she was really nasty and up her own butt. I soon cut her down to size. I told her if I spoke to my audience like she spoke to me, I'd be through the door.

8 September 2013

Gabe and me were invited tonight to the Orangery in Margam Park. The show was called 'A Night at the Musicals' and my dear friend, Beverley Humphreys was hosting it. Adam Robert Lewis put the show together. A newcomer to me, he's stepped into the limelight, as he was once a graphic designer but now sings songs from the shows. He had previously arranged his début show in London to high acclaim. They were also joined by West End star Katy Treharne. The show was in a beautiful Roman setting with pillars and posh drapes. Adam opened with 'I am what I am', so I was away with the fairies and the show went rather well. The duets were good and Beverley Humphreys was out of this world. There were two little mishaps. Katy walked off the stage after her song and nearly knocked one of the pillars over. You could say she brought the house down – nearly! And, at one point, Beverley's microphone stand fell over, crashing to the floor. It made the whole thing look as if it was oh, so very real. Yes, things do happen, even in the world of wonderful show business.

I've known Beverley for years, not only as a colleague but as a fan, too. As the years have rolled on I've grown to admire her even more. Her programme, *Beverley's World of Music*, has to be one of my favourites on Radio Wales. Usually I listen to her show on the way home from a live concert. I think it has to be said that I'm addicted to her varied choice of music and her broadcasting voice. I often comment on her radio show. Once I phoned her up at home and she was so thrilled that I'd taken the time to call her and basically rave about her show. She was delighted that a Doctor of Music was a great fan of hers. She's so very humble, such a true lady and such an asset to Radio Wales.

So many people knew who I was and people came to speak to me in their droves. I wore some new clothes – you can't beat new. You don't get any food spots on new clothes out of the packet. I had quite a shock as we walked into the Orangery. Gabe said, "Look at your arm," and so I did and there was a label on my sleeve saying machine washable. It was stitched on the bottom of the sleeve. Gabe got it off. Good job I cut the price tag off. That was a mistake, trust me.

I turned out to be the chief raffle man. I drew the raffle – anything for a front seat!

↕

My life at the moment is so wrong. I'm arguing with the people around me and telling them where to go, but then people around me are so bloody nasty and jealous. I would say I tell at least half a dozen people a day to sling their hooks. And it's really so out of character for me, but I have to stand up for myself. It all stems from success and having money and a better life than most. Well I'm sorry, but I'm not giving my achievements up for anybody. If you want something, go and work for it. I'm just wondering what Monday will bring. I'm still living in rubble and crap, with no shower, hot water or heating. Oh yes, and no carpet in the kitchen. When the assessor came out some weeks ago, he tore up half the floor covering as it was badly water damaged and stained from the ceiling collapse. He mentioned that if it was left in that state, it would only deteriorate and become a health hazard. So, now I'm left with a health and safety hazard which we keep tripping over the end he cut off, even though he placed masking tape on the raised edge.

Sunday night and another weekend is over. I'm going to bed now to dream of Spain. In my dream I'm going to be tanned, tall and slim and above all, Spanish. Good night, *buenas noches, carino* xxx.

Here we go. It's 4.30 a.m. and I'm sat on the bed on a Monday morning wishing for a massive change in life. I don't want to be in Cwmafan; it's too far for work every night. I hate travelling back in the early hours and feeling so tired. I want to be in Cardiff. If I go back to Cardiff, I'd be on my own. I'd see Gabe for an hour a day before I left for work, like in the old days, and the same for Buster; he'd never get to see Gabe either. Gabe would have to commute daily from Cardiff to Cwmafan and that would cost an extra £500 per month. And it wouldn't be worth paying the extra out. So, in my current state of mind, I'm a prisoner and I'm not happy with that situation as I'm a free bird by right. So I have to try and sleep and face another day here, and just miss Cardiff and Spain like mad.

It wouldn't be so bad if people left me alone, but I've got no chance of that. Everywhere else I'm treated with respect as a radio personality but here, where I was brought up, I'm constantly questioned about things that don't concern them. Are people just getting nosier? Maybe I'm getting much more reserved as I get older. I want and need some privacy. It was the lack of privacy and respect that drove us away from the village some years ago. We lived at the house my mother left me part of the week, and I reopened the shops opposite. But Gabe would constantly be locking the front door because he got fed up of people just walking in without knocking first, walking straight through the dining room into the kitchen before calling out. He'd get annoyed if he was in the bathroom, or just lying on the bed, resting or cooking. This time around, it's different as the door is always locked as we have Buster to think of.

At that time, I wanted to sell up everything I had but, of course, there was the credit crunch and financial downturn. So I couldn't sell then because I'd lose a fortune as I'd upgraded so much and, although things have improved recently, it's still not good. So that contributes to me feeling like a prisoner. I know that my mother never expected me to live in the village and, if I am honest, she would have expected me to have sold up immediately. My mother always said, "Do what you bloody want. People will have a go at you anyway." How right she was. The more you give the less you get thought of, but if I do sell up, will I sell my parents' house as well? Something I will have to think hard about.

9 September 2013

Gabe said last night that I'd never go to Spain to live, that I only keep talking about it, but I'm afraid that's wrong. I've got one foot in the airport right now. I have to buy a place really soon and then I have to price furniture removal companies. I'm hoping I can do my programme from Spain. Well, others do. I've been looking online for apartments in Spain for me, Gabe and Buster. I'd prefer a villa to be honest. I'll see what's about. It's fun living in cuckoo-land and I love it there, but I'm very determined to have a place abroad again. I can't wait to step off British soil and frazzle in Hispanic climes.

I'm still waiting to see if the BBC has decided to commission my TV programme in their schedules. I hope they do but, if they decide against it, I'll probably refuse to do any more pilot shows. It's really disheartening to have them rejected. All the previous ones have been genuinely well received but, like the tapes, I feel I've been shelved too. What would be the point of doing another one?

I'm planning another trip to Spain as I'm running out of soap! I only use the green Spanish soap made from olives. Well that's my excuse, and I'm sticking to it. The charity shop has run out of 'black' soap as well, so I need to get more stock of that at the same time.

Just discovered that after having a new ceiling installed, the plumber checking the shower also looked at the boiler, made some alterations and the new pressure blew some joints in the central heating system and water has started pouring through the new ceiling! So now I have no shower, hot water, or central heating and a new water-stained ceiling! What was I saying about people and their work? I don't know where to turn.

12 September 2013

It's been a month since the new schedules started. Gabe's on the phones tonight, but I can't attract his attention as he's so busy. The new four-hour show is working well and the return of the Daisy chain has been well received; that's where if a listener gets the answer to a question right, he or she has to set the next question and so on. BBC Radio Wales are also updating my page on their website. It lists the questions asked and the answers, and who set the new question. It's all good at the moment, all the new and revived features, but it's taxing my brain big time trying to think of new ideas to keep the show sounding fresh. I suppose that's a good thing, though.

I'm off to London to have my throat checked soon and I might have to be there for two days now. Mind you, there's always the shopping. I'll put up with a bit of shopping! It's been an experience, these last three years, what with the illness and the massive weight loss. It's so difficult being in the public eye and ill. I've apparently supposedly had Aids, leukaemia, prostrate cancer, lung cancer, throat cancer, testicular cancer – the list goes on and on. The general public can be so inventive. I constantly have to reassert that I just had a bad reaction to prescribed drugs. So me and tablets have just had a divorce – a massive one.

Someone asked me, "When do I feel good and safe and happy?" I reckon it's when I've got some good things happening, like a massive concert or maybe a new programme on TV or radio, when I'm busy. That makes me feel good. OK, a trip to Spain is always welcome. Shopping in London is a wonderful experience. Like I've said before, have you ever tried to kit yourself out in Port Talbot? Virtually impossible – no silk shirts! Regent and Oxford Streets are wonderful. And as for being safe, it's when I'm sat on my bed with the door locked, and I'm in my nightshirt. Wonderful.

I think I've come to a decision. I've been planning in my mind what to do when I go to Spain for good. First of all I won't go till I'm 65. There, I've said it. Then, I just need to perform a bit and maybe do a programme or two on the wireless. The rest of the time I want to sit in the sun and frazzle. It still doesn't mean I won't be going to other places – can you imagine me without a passport!

Chapter 17

13 September 2013

Last night I was sat in the studio doing my programme and one of the security men came in to speak to Gabe on the other side of the glass partition. I could sense that something was wrong. The message was brought to me and I was right. It was from my old mate, Ronnie Huxford. He was my drummer for years and a damn good one, too. He'd played with just about every outfit there was. I worked with Ronnie at the White Wheat club in Maesteg for years. That's where he met his wife, Janice. There was a big age gap. Ronnie was always vague about the figures but hey, they were mega happy together and that's all that mattered. I saw them both frequently over the years and they had a son called little Ronnie. I always tried to be there as a friend for them when things got rough, and in the entertainment business that wasn't unusual for any of us. But, as a couple, they were truly happy. So many said their marriage wouldn't last because of the age difference, but they proved them all wrong and, more to the point, the romance lasted too.

Back to the phone call. It was Ronnie on the phone telling us that Janice had died. I was so saddened, and this was in the middle of my programme. God help him. He was so lost on the phone that night. We'd always wondered how Janice would cope if she was left alone, how much support she'd need from friends and family. It gave us the chance to reminisce on happier times.

Ronnie and Janice came to a birthday party I was holding

at the flats in Cardiff and I'll never forget something Janice did. She was holding a drink and went to sit on a stool, misjudged where it was, and fell. She landed on the floor, on her bottom, sat upright and her glass was still intact with not a drop spilt. We talked about that for years. Ronnie says he's in his 80s now – and he's still playing the drums. Music *does* keep you young. God bless you, Ron.

14 September 2013

This weekend is over before it began, or so it seems. The show at the Riverfront Theatre in Newport was exceptional.

I love to go out into the foyer after each show to meet the audience and make certain that they've enjoyed their evening. I always encourage all the other performers to join me as well as this makes the experience complete, particularly if someone has travelled far or they've difficulties in getting about – it's maybe one of the few times they're able to socialise or make new friends. At the Riverfront show the audience was eager to see us. Rob Allen was there, in full cowboy attire and sang some of his own country songs. He is an old Garden favourite and everyone loves him. Dame Mandy Starr was also on the bill. She'd just lost her father two days earlier and I was worried in case she couldn't sing. But, like the trouper that she is, she was there. And the incredible thing was that she was asked to sing 'O Mio Babbino Caro' – Oh My Beloved Father in English – and she did, and she was filling up on stage while singing it. The audience was sobbing as well. It was such a moving night. I walked on the stage and hugged her and she broke her heart. She is truly a great professional.

But, as always, I was glad to get home and have chips in the house with Gabe and Buster. I'm forever asking Gabe "Did I do OK? Did anyone walk out? Do you think I offended anyone by not meeting them?" I'm so drained after a show; I seem to be in such a mess.

↕

I'm sat in my bed at 6.30 in the morning. And I don't want to be here. I wish I could leave here today. Bad memories are winning again. How do I get over this feeling? I can't seek counselling as I'm called the 'great Chris Needs' and 'Chris puts everybody to right', so how can I show weakness? It's a difficult one.

I turn on the TV and what's on? Sport. I just hope the day gets better.

The diabetes is not good. As long as Gabe will scatter me in Spain I'll be a happy corpse. At the moment I can't think of anything else but Spain. I wish now that I'd never gone there in the first place. Little did I know that, when I stepped off that plane, I'd be opening a can of worms. What would I be like if I was just a British-orientated person? I'd have probably died by now of boredom. Playing pool and ducking and dodging rain isn't my thing. I just want to wear a T-shirt for a living, and sit on the beach – but you already know that!

I'm just wondering what the *Come the Revolution* programme is going to be like. As I've already mentioned, it's Chris Corcoran's show that was recorded at the BBC Club a few weeks back. I was a little wild and mega camp. But hey, that's me! I still find it hard to condone my attitude about being openly gay, as it's still a crime in the back of my mind after all the years of being told and dictated to by teachers that I was a freak, and that I'd end up in prison or a special hospital for mental patients. It was, at one time, discussed in school that I should be kept away from other pupils as I might be a bad influence on them!

↕

One thing which has always stayed with me is the first time that I saw Gibraltar as we approached it by car on the road from Malaga. As you go around the bend, it almost falls on top of you, and hits you. It's so magnificent, it's unbelievable. But having said all that, it's Spain I want more than anywhere else. Gabe wants Gibraltar, so I can see an argument brewing.

The fascinating part of Gibraltar is the frontier. I remember when I worked in Sotogrande, I'd go for a drive down to the frontier just to have a nose at the Rock. But in those days the frontier was closed up. I used to see people shouting through the gates, things like "Hey, Maria your sister's had a baby" and so forth. I remember seeing the British bobbies patrolling on the other side and there was, of course, the red British phone boxes. It was so strange to see all of this. What was Britain doing stuck on the end of Spain? Or is it the other way round? I immediately started studying up on the Rock.

Later, in about 1982, I was there when they reopened the frontier, and floods of people passed through. It looked like the dismantling of the Berlin Wall. There were tears, smiles and hugs and a lot of people in high spirits. That's something I'll never forget, and it will stay with me forever. Initially, the frontier was only open for Spanish citizens or inhabitants of Gibraltar to cross. It was 1985 before the gates were officially opened to all tourists, cars and commercial traffic. The town, La Linea, which is the first bit of Spanish soil you step onto as you leave Gibraltar, was very run down. They used to have potholes in the roads that were so big you could ruin your car if you went into one. But now, after all these years, La Linea has done well for itself. It's no longer a provincial village but has become really posh and has many opportunities for people living there, and the potholes have gone! I wish I could say the same for here in Wales!

They have a McDonald's takeaway just on the Spanish side and what is funny is that they have a licensed bar there as well. Could you imagine if that was the situation here in the UK? Now we all know what the Brits are like when they go abroad; we've seen the TV programmes made about the drunks etc. I reckon if bars were put in fast-food places here, there'd be people strewn about everywhere in car parks and on the roads. The evidence is there isn't it when you see Brits abroad. With the exception of a few, I suppose, there are still some people left that can drink and be sensible.

When I worked out in Spain for all those years, I was more or less like a Spanish person. I worked with them, I spoke their language, I was invited to their fiestas etc. and I loved their way of life. My mother always said that she must have had an encounter with a Spaniard because I was always more suited to Spain than Wales. I listened to what the Spanish would say when the younger British crowd would descend on Benidorm during August. The police would have extra men on patrol as a result. At night, after work, me and the Spanish waiters would sit out the front having a drink and a bite to eat, and we would watch the young Brits screaming, falling over, throwing up, and breaking trees. I felt so let down. One waiter asked me if I was from the same place as them. And I said yes. What more could I say? The number of youngsters who asked me to translate for them to get them out of jail was incredible. They were like little lambs in the morning, in sick-covered T-shirts. Why did they do all that nonsense? Was it because of the fantastic weather or the large alcohol measures, or maybe they felt as if they were let out of prison with all of the restrictions in the UK, e.g. drink up and get out, it's time to close at 3.30 p.m? So, of course, abroad, when the juice of holiday mood is flowing, the trouble starts. Mind you, the Spanish are so used to having the drink flowing that they just think nothing of it.

Now that the licensing laws have been relaxed here in the UK, has it got any better? I'll let you answer that one. I know one thing; like many others, I'm too frightened to walk alone in a British city on a Friday or Saturday night. I'm really scared.

One thing that fascinated me about France and Spain was that children were sat in bars and restaurants and were given alcohol, admittedly in small amounts and much diluted. But, who knows, there may be a knock-on effect.

I've had an idea. I want to turn a room in one of my homes into a sunroom with a solarium and I want to put sand on the floor. I wonder if that would work. I could lie there and close my eyes and play some holiday music and pretend. Once, many years ago, I laid a lawn in my living room. But the grass didn't live. I must be off my head!

↕

If you asked what I enjoy immensely, it's the stage work, particularly when out and about on the road as with the BBC Summer Scorcher tour. OK, it often did rain quite a bit, but the entertainment was good. I worked with Rob Allen and the Garden song was written. We raised quite a bit for charity with that song and it's still being played on the radio today. Mandy Starr was a great part of the show too, and has become so popular over the years and a huge Garden favourite. Back in the early days of the Garden, before any financial downturn, things were so very, very good. Morale was high and so were budgets. The sky was the limit. There was so much fun and friendship to be had.

I remember flying off to Jersey for a weekend with Gabe and on the same plane was Mary Yeoman, a Garden member. Well, we just hit it off and we even went to Guernsey together, me and Gabe and her and her hubby, Gwyn. It was a great time and I remember shopping with Mary and fancying a watch. Then, at a later date, when I was performing at a theatre, Mary came on the stage and presented me with a dual time zone watch (a double-faced watch as I called it) and a considerable amount of money for the charity. She'd been secretly arranging a collection from all the Garden members who'd been attending my various shows and events. The Garden has always supported me and my charity events and I regard them all as true friends.

Yes, those were the days. I think it all started going downhill when the BBC put a stop to the questions, competitions and quizzes, not only on my programme but across the whole BBC broadcasting network at that time. And, all because of some bloody nonsense in London. Now, bear in mind, none of this was my fault, but I had to pay the price. In the end I was frightened even to ask "How are you?" in case it presented itself as a question. The show suffered and there was nothing I could do about it. Or was there?

I'd had enough one day, so I made an appointment to see one of the top management people on the third floor of the BBC. I put a suit on and off I went with fury in my heart. I went for it big time and then, just as I was getting to the climax of my argument, I said the same thing again in Welsh. That always goes down well! I was evil and rightly so, and obviously very, very loud. I stepped out into the main office to a round of applause from the staff at their desks. I'd been completely unaware I could be overheard, or how much of a nerve I'd hit.

The rules were relaxed a little and, eventually, I got back the right to ask some questions; of course, long after the London broadcasters got their quizzes back, but I was on the road again. The thing is, I never went into broadcasting to have a war, but it certainly felt like it. The show has had a new lease of life and I truly believe that my new boss, Steve, has done the right thing in re-launching my Garden. It's too good a thing to throw away. A lot of people depend on it and need it. Me included.

I remember back over the last 17 years, and a lot of different BBC bosses have passed through. Some were really good but, of course, some not so. I'm glad to say that I survived the stormy patches and I'm still here to moan and groan about the weather. At one point I'd had a guts-full of crazy bosses and bad decisions and then I heard that a colleague of mine from Touch AM Radio, which was an independent radio station in Cardiff, was applying for the job. I just hoped he'd be successful in getting the position because I liked him and, more importantly, I believed in him and trusted him. It didn't happen straight away but, on the next occasion, I was routeing for him. I called him at home one night, just before I was going on air in Llandaff, and I told him that I really hoped he'd get the job as editor and that I was crossing fingers for him and anything else I could cross. I just wanted him to get the number one job because he breathes, eats and lives radio. I think he knew then (but didn't show me – maybe I'm wrong) that he was successful. I was really pleased for him. But, don't get me wrong, we've had our ups and downs and I've made mistakes, but I'm honest with him and he believes in the Garden. He's pretty fair with me (most of the time) and me to him also (honest!). I would do anything for Radio Wales as a radio station, even though I've had some ups and downs with the BBC. The Beeb is a big business, and so you have to sail down the river with it, whatever direction it goes, but my show on Radio Wales is my baby and I'd climb Mount Everest for it in my mobility scooter. (OK, you could say I'm dedicated!)

When I first started at the BBC it was like entering a new city. It was massive; I didn't even know where the toilets were. The people were so different to what I was used to. There were producers for a start, something I'd never encountered before. What did a radio producer do? I'd always paddled my own canoe. I tried to befriend people there but found it quite hard at the beginning. Some producers and staff were a bit insular and thought that I was very much the new boy and still very 'independent radio' minded. I'd set my sights high and there was a long way to go.

One person I targeted was Alan Thompson. To be honest, I found Alan in the very early days quite distant. Some said he was shy. I have to be honest I don't believe in shyness – I call it the 'I don't want to know' syndrome. I bumped into him now and then, but we never really became bosom buddies. Alan and me did the odd road show and handover at four o'clock when my afternoon show led into his drivetime show.

But it all changed between us when I was introduced to his mother. What a fabulous lady! Full of fun, a real genuine lady and she loved the Garden programme, especially in the early days. As the years went on, Madeleine (Lyn), me and especially Gabe became great friends. When I then spoke to Alan it was always "My mother loves you" etc. and as we spoke more and more, we became good mates too. My sexuality never seemed to bother him at all, and certainly not his mother. His mam and

I started to exchange jokes. Alan will tell you that his mother had the sense of humour of a docker. We always laughed and exchanged dozens of jokes. If you spoke to Lyn you'd think you were talking to royalty. Alan told me that the posh voice was her broadcasting/chatting voice. I sent Lyn a DVD of my show at the Swansea Grand Theatre because she was unable to attend; Alan would relay messages from his mam to tell me how much she loved the stage show and all of my CDs. So it was Lyn, Alan's mam, which brought me and Alan together. Today we are great, great friends. I call to see Alan every night and give him some chocolates from my studio. We laugh and joke and compare our mothers, as there were a lot of similarities with the both of them.

I did a programme with Alan, *By Royal Appointment*. He's very good with dry humour, while I'm an open book and, as I've said, more like Bernard Manning. Alan would hand over every night to the Garden show and always make sure that we had a bit of a laugh. I would always ask Lyn, when she came on the programme for a chat, "How's mummy's little soldier?" referring, of course, to Alan. When it came to birthdays, I would send Lyn some saucy cards and but the ones she'd send me back were much worse but so funny.

When I became ill Alan was there for me. I'd go into his studio even though I was so weak I felt that I was going to die. Alan was so supportive and almost nursed me, as some nights I'd be in tears. As I started to improve, Alan and me became even closer. The next shock I got was that his mam Lyn had died. Alan was devastated.

He and his mam were amazing friends. I felt so bad for Alan as I knew exactly how he was feeling as I'd also lost my mother. What could I do? Nothing, except support him, even if it was only a chat and a cuppa. Gabe and me attended Lyn's funeral. We closed the shop and, to be honest, wild horses wouldn't have kept us away. It was all very moving and I was almost driven to tears in the church.

Alan started to pick up the pieces of his life and returned to his programme and I'd pop in with biscuits etc. trying to keep his pecker up, and then another bombshell was dropped. His evening show came to an end and he was once again devastated. What could I do? He was so upset that even when I popped in to see if he was OK the two of us just lost the plot. A little while later, he was offered the late show on a Sunday. The slot at the time was being filled by my 'Best Bits' of the week. There was no-one more pleased than me; I was so chuffed for Alan. We're as close as anyone could be. He's a dear friend.

$$\updownarrow$$

I reckon that the security guys at the BBC are probably my best mates in the building. We're always helping each other out. I give them cakes and I get a good parking place! Hey, what more can I ask for? When I was on the weekend breakfast show, I used to sit in their office in the early morning and they'd keep me going with tea and try to wake me up.

Once, in the afternoon, I was outside having a fag and this fella came and stood next to me, dressed quite oddly. I thought he was an actor in costume. Although standing by me, he didn't acknowledge me at all. I thought that he might be a bit of a 'stuck-up lovey'. The next thing, he went into reception and took out a massive sword-like weapon and attacked one of the security guards, slicing his head with this sword thing. The others were quick to react and they got him onto the floor and gaffer-taped him. I'm not sure what the problem was, but if you're not fussed about a BBC programme, just write in for goodness sake! It might have just been a bad programme, I thought. But hey, who knows anything about anyone! My mother always said, "You can live with someone for 50 years and still not know them." I suppose there's some method or madness in that somewhere. Generally, I get on well with the boys on the door. I'm quite a Jack the lad and they've been pretty good to me.

One night, driving back home, I noticed there was someone

following behind me, flashing their lights now and again. I wondered if it was just my vivid imagination, but who was this? So I turned off the road in another direction and the car followed me. Nope, no imagination, they were definitely following me. I immediately phoned Gabe on my hands-free and asked him where he was. He was working away at the time, half asleep and didn't really understand what I was going on about. He told me that he was in a hotel in Pembroke and I'd just woken him up. I asked him if he was having me followed. He simply said, "You must be off your head." No, he wasn't having me followed. So I turned round and went back the way I came. And still the car followed me. So then I got back to the BBC and then the car disappeared. I studied this situation for a few weeks and then decided to report it. But I wanted to be sure and not appear to be a twit. You see, although I'd only spotted the car occasionally and at a distance, I'd had sweets put through the door of my house in Cwmafan and notes sent to me at the BBC saying what time my lights went off and how this person (a woman apparently) was going to change me. Christ, she'd have a job on! Simple cow! I told the BBC and my boss Julie was brilliant. The police were informed and a panic button was given to me, but nobody knew how to set it up. The police came to my home and set it up in case the woman/freak came there. (Hell, if she could iron, I'd let her in – JOKE!)

We were living mainly just outside Bridgend at that time, next door to the police chief constable, so the area was well watched anyway, I reckon. One night after I left for work, Gabe phoned me. He was at home watching *Coronation Street* and the alarm went off. A silent alarm. There were Black Marias everywhere. It was like *The Streets of San Francisco*. The woman was never caught; she was as clever and as shrewd as they came. I reckon she finally gave up. Anyone that wanted an encounter with me must have had severe problems. I don't even want to be me, let alone go out with me!

I still get freaks writing to me – sometimes on paper or sometimes in a card. The last card said 'die queer' on it but the card itself was nice, fair play. People ask me why I want to do a runner. I just want a normal life.

Being a gay man, I've always got on with girls and thought nothing of it when I was introduced to a particular singer. She was eager to get on; she came to visit me and was adamant that she wanted to be on the stage and radio scene. I offered her some work in theatre shows, remembering that theatre work is very hard to come by. From the word go she had her head in the clouds. People were asking me "Who does she think she is?" because she was welcoming the audience to *her* show, virtually insinuating that I was supporting her – more than annoying when, in reality, she only *my* guest artiste. I was constantly asked what was I going to do with her and was advised to get rid of her but me, true to my word, battled on hoping to find the good in someone. It never happened, I have to admit. She was the star and I was nothing.

One night she walked off stage and went home. When I approached her about this she screamed at me "Everything is you, you, you." "Well," I said, "it is my show." She then went on to tell me that I was an embarrassment to be seen with. Mind you, that statement was after she'd earned a fortune compared to her clubland life. I have to admit that after meeting someone as horrible as her, it nearly put me off women permanently. I've never seen someone so star-struck and seen greed and jealousy take over a person as much as her in my life – and I've met a few over the years. So much so that I will not trust another 'up and coming' girl near me, for fear of it happening again.

Since then she's married someone rich and is living abroad. I saw that one coming a mile off and so did just about everyone that came into contact with her, so they told me. You're never too old to learn, nor are you too old to be used. Why are people like that I ask myself, and it has to be jealousy. It can't be anything else. Sad. I wonder who she's taking for a ride now?

Chapter 18

30 September 2013

I was at Llanelli's Ffwrnes Theatre last night – a stunning venue – with Llanelli Male Voice Choir who kindly donated their services free to the charity, along with Carole Rees Jones and Tammi Rae Bois (Tammi 'the phones' on my radio show).

Carole Rees Jones did really well, her singing was spot on and she excelled herself. I went on stage to thank her and take her off before introducing the next artistes. As always, she was glamorous, just like Dorothy Squires at the Palladium, all plumes and feathers. But, as she walked off, her heel caught in the feathers that were dragging on the floor. I had my back to her at the time and the next thing I heard was an almighty crash. I turned around and there she was on the floor with her butt in the air. She'd fallen over and the audience gave an almighty gasp. I helped her up but she had to take her shoes off first.

I told the audience she'd be all right as long as she didn't fall for me. There was a laugh, but we could all see that she'd had quite a bump. I looked at her heels and they were like stilts. I could've cleaned the upstairs window wearing them. But she was OK. She came back to my house and we had some supper and then she left for the airport to go to Spain. Jammy cow!

I've known Tammi Rae Bois since she was 13 years old. She has danced at my stage shows and then she'd also come into the BBC and take to the phones on my programme. She could work just about every machine in my studio but, as she was only 16 years old then, she had to wait patiently until she was 18 before she could apply for a job at the BBC in Cardiff. She then ventured upstairs as a broadcast assistant, and is now well and truly established at the Beeb. Tammi was cast as the fairy and sang beautifully in Owen Money's recent pantos. When I found that out we later chatted about her doing a few of my stage shows, not as a dancer but as a soubrette. She sang in Llanelli and stormed the place with her songs and her tap dancing. Tammi is very talented young lady, with a genuine personality and I feel she has big future in entertainment.

It all comes out when I'm shopping

I'm always shopping. I must have shares in smoked bacon, that's all I seem to buy. As I'm getting older the shopping trolley seems to change into a Zimmer frame. I have my man bag in the child's seat and my heavy-duty shopping bags in the front of the trolley in the little compartment; a place for everything and everything in its place. And off I go like a bat up a chimney. I try to go up and down every single aisle because I'm not organised enough to make a list – that's in my head. But my memory retention has weakened somewhat. (I wish I could forget my childhood.) So I have to study what's on each aisle to see if I need it. Then I'm always buying bargains whether I need them or not. I have dishwasher tablets coming out of my ears. But when I'm out and about, and don't get me wrong because I do appreciate it, I'm stopped in nearly every aisle, often by an elderly lady, so I make a fuss. We have a chat and have a laugh and I always thank them for listening as without them I'd be nothing. Then we part company and I stand there in the first aisle wondering what the bloody hell I was looking for. It takes me an age to shop.

In Asda's in Cardiff Bay, Debbie, the official 'welcomer' to the store, is always on the microphone. She once came over to ask me why I'd been 25 minutes in the first aisle and if I was all right. Debbie knew how ill I'd been and kept an eye on me in my bad days. What a nice lady. Thank you, Debbs.

Thinking about the past

My Auntie Hilary, my father's sister, was one of the nicest people I've ever met in my life. I have to be honest, we – as in all of us – are not a close family. In fact, we never see each other from one decade to the next. But going back about 50 years, I was always back and forth to my Auntie Hilary's. Honestly, she was an angel and she gave me the world.

I remember once, in her home near Aberafan beach, we were celebrating a birthday. We only had a radio – there were no CDs and things like that then. So we put the radio on to have a dance. All we could find on the radio was talking. So my auntie started dancing to someone saying jokes on the wireless. She said, "I hope he'll start saying faster jokes so I can have a jive later."

She had two daughters, Nicole and Lisa. I haven't seen the girls for yonks, but now and then I do see Lisa and she's lovely with me. I'm not used to having family being nice to me. She works in a hospital and she's the younger of the two. She keeps asking me to come down to the hospital to meet the patients as they all listen to my Garden show. But every time I go she's not there. Bad luck or timing, I reckon. But she's a lovely girl, just like her mam. She greets me with such a fuss and I'm so happy that someone in my family is pleased to see me.

Gabe and me were on our way out of Aberafan shopping centre the other day and I saw this woman walking towards me and she smiled and said, "Hello Christopher." Now nobody calls me Christopher, more's the pity, and I stopped in my tracks. "Nicole?" I asked in surprise and, indeed, it was her. She looked like my auntie, yet again. We talked and reminisced. One thing that will never leave me was the day that me, Auntie Hilary and Nicole went to Afan Lido. We were walking along the front of the complex and there were pools of goldfish outside with stepping stones to walk across. Me and Nicole tried jumping the stones and guess what? … Yes, Nicole fell in. My auntie was so embarrassed that she walked off and left me and Nicole to it. I pulled Nicole out of the fish pool and couldn't find Auntie Hilary anywhere. She'd gone back to my nana's house. She was as red as a beetroot. But all was OK – Nicole dried out wonderfully!

I'm talking here about my family and I don't know how to cope with it. I've never had any sort of relationship with my family. We're all very distant or, more truthfully, just don't speak to each other. I think that if I was invited to lunch or dinner by a member of my remaining close family, I'd have a heart attack with the shock.

↕

I've just had to ask Gabe to send more paperwork to my accountant. Stuff to Companies House like rate reviews and company surveys have to be done by law, and all by a certain date.

I just wish they'd put more lights on in our street. I've tripped over so many times simply because I can't see the curb of the pavement! Just one of my many gripes!

I've also just sent my column off to the *Golwg* magazine – I've written this for many years. I enjoy it to be honest. It's all in Welsh but it keeps my Welsh language going. I don't do as much as I used to these days, which is a pity.

There's so much going on at the moment, I don't know where to turn. Most of it is red tape. I can't believe how much red tape there is in business today. It's all getting me down, to be honest. So I've decided that if I can't go to live in Spain right now, this very minute, then I'll have to resort to Plan B. I hear you ask "What might that be then?" I'm going to have to go to Spain twice a month, on the weekends, at least, otherwise I'll go crackers being here all the time.

The dawning of Aquarius

Aquarius was a group I joined in 1972 at the Townsman Club which, at that time, was one of the biggest nightclubs in Swansea. I was 17 and still at school. I did the odd organ-playing job at the Townsman and when Aquarius was looking for a keyboard player, Derek Wignal, the owner, suggested me. So off I went in my school uniform for an audition with the band. My God, this was a massive thing for me to do, but I wanted the bright lights. I went in my orange Mini, parked up, and walked towards the door of the club. Little did I know that this was where my life would change forever. I went in and saw other keyboard players auditioning for the job and thought, being so young, that I didn't stand a chance.

It was my turn and I had to read music and accompany the female singer. I remember the drummer, who seemed to be the spokesman, saying under his breath, "Bloody hell, this boy's good!" But I was told that they'd let me know in about a week. Of course, I was crawling up the walls and I was over at the Townsman every night with friends, hoping that the band would inform me when they saw me at the club. But no! I waited and waited and eventually I asked the lady singer, who I addressed as Mrs Haynes (Aileen) – did she know anything? She said that the men in the band would be speaking to me shortly. I was approached by Phil, Reg and Barry (Aileen's husband) and they simply said that I was the best they'd seen in donkey's years and that they'd be thrilled to have me in the band.

My God, it was like I'd just won the pools! I phoned my mother and when I told her she simply said, "...as the song says, 'Baby, it had to be you'," and started to sing it to me. She was such a big fan of mine I have to admit, the biggest fan ever.

Phil and Reg were Aileen's brothers. Phil played the lead guitar and Reg played the bass. They were so unalike to look at; Phil looked a bit like Roy Orbison with the dark hair and glasses and Reg was very thin and had fairer hair. When on stage playing their instruments they'd chat to each other in between songs. But, strangely, they'd call each other Harry. I was so bloody naive that I asked them why did their parents' name both of them the same. Later I found out that Harry was just a nickname.

Aquarius was at its peak then, learning new songs on a regular basis. I had a list of rehearsals with the band to learn dance numbers and I got to accompany many big names: Faith Brown, Roger Whittaker, The Baron Knights, Jimmy Helms... the stars were endless. I have to be honest, the two brothers helped me learn about the whole industry, showing me the ropes, learning all the technical terms and everything in between. I was getting known in Swansea big time, and I used to go out for meals with the band some nights and then with the owners of the club, the Wignals, at other times. They were so good to me; they bought me a new keyboard and PA system, and looked after me like I was royalty.

I sometimes went over to the casino in the High Street and had a quid on the blackjack, but no more. I was too frightened of what I saw going on there. People were losing money and getting drunk and then coming back the following night to try and win it back. I steered clear of this as I wasn't going to lose my hard-earned cash. But I did enjoy the company. I felt important and not as threatened as I was in Cwmafan.

I grew up fast in Swansea, and became close to Aileen, Barry, Phil and Reg. They all got on well with my family and, to be honest, they were truly like a second family to me and treated me like their kid brother. I loved it all and was included in every occasion.

They also loved Spain and asked me to join them there on a three-week trip to Pineda de Mar. I accepted and had a great time. I guess this holiday spoilt me; it was the first time I'd been to Spain. It was my first holiday abroad without my parents, too! Their family, their mam and dad and the rest, were already living in Spain and, fair play, I was treated well and got to know them. While on holiday Phil had an accident. He was a sleepwalker and one night he sleepwalked off the balcony. How he survived I'll never know, but he did, thank God. He was lucky to be alive. They reckoned that he broke nearly every bone in his body and he did look a mess. He probably survived because of his family's love. They were so close and Phil lived to play another guitar gig. Phil married Sue and Reg married Brenda and all their children looked on me as Uncle Chris which I loved, as my own family never really bothered with me, with the exception of my mother.

As the years went by we did well but, like everything else, it came to an end. The band went to Spain to live permanently and I ventured off to one of the biggest workmen's club in south Wales – Taibach and Port Talbot Working Men's Club and Institute. I soon became 'kingpin' there and I earned the reputation of being one of the best organists in Wales and maybe further afield. Singers would bring their best and most difficult arrangements with them and I loved those challenges and the attention. Me and Aquarius kept in touch and it still felt like a family affair. Barry and Aileen came to my first TV show, *Showcase*, on HTV Wales and I often popped to see Phil and his wife Sue in Swansea as they were still living in Wales.

Sadly Phil died a few years ago. Apparently he went to the doctor suffering from a bad stomach; he was sent for tests and they told him he only had a short time to live. I was devastated, but he'd reached the point of acceptance, kept telling me jokes and laughing as on any previous time we'd met up. He planned his own funeral which, of course, I attended. Lots of rock and roll music. It was so unfair, so young and talented and he had a beautiful family. It took me a long time to get over that, to be honest.

Barry and Aileen came back from Spain to live in Suffolk and they arranged to call to see me in Cardiff. A further bombshell. Barry revealed that he, too, was very ill. We kept in touch by phone but, when Barry died, I felt it all too much. Like Phil, he was so young but had been suffering for months. Unfortunately I couldn't get to that funeral as it was in Suffolk.

The next thing, Sue called me to let me know that Aileen was ill and a little while later I received a call from Sue and Phil's daughter, Hannah, to tell me that Aileen had died.

Of my 'showbiz' family, there's only Reg left. He and his wife Brenda and their children are still living in Neath. I got in touch with them as I hadn't seen them for years and I felt it was the right thing to do.

They recently came along to my show in Porthcawl. I reckon it must have been a big shock for them to see me with my Garden following, doing well and known everywhere. The show was fabulous and when I went to see Reg at the end, there were genuine tears in his eyes. I think he felt it when I sang 'I am what I am'. He knew first-hand what I'd been through, the pain, suffering and ridicule I had to take growing up. He simply said, "You've won kid!"

There are a lot of Aquarius's children and their families that I haven't seen for years. I'm going to make an effort to see them all if I can. They are my extended family and all too good to miss out on. After all they came from fantastic stock. God bless you Aquarius. You certainly put me on the right road, including introducing me to Spain and the continental way of life and I thank you for that, all of it, until the day I die.

Chapter 19

Llinos, what can I say about the girl of my dreams? I was called to a meeting with the editor of Radio Wales to discuss the new scheduling for the station. New procedures and compliance meant that I'd now have a production team and I was advised that these positions would go out to tender. I was pleased, as this only confirmed the popularity of the show and gave it some security – well, as far as any contract could. But I also had my reservations. I couldn't work with anyone I wasn't happy with. I was also concerned that there'd be interference. I mean, after all, why alter what isn't broke. I had a successful format and I achieved that without a production team. It was me and a telephone answerer – did I need anyone else?

The company which landed the contract, Terrier Productions, was headed by Llinos Jones. I was so pleased because I knew her and we got on like a house on fire, but I still had my reservations. There was a lot to learn for the both of us. The important thing was that we really got on well and that I placed my trust in her wholeheartedly. Whatever I needed or wanted, Llinos just got on with it. I became her priority and she tries her utmost to make me number one. I couldn't ask for any more.

When I started my radio show I did everything: I answered the phones myself, set the questions, did the paperwork, answered letters and put people in the Garden. Now I just walk in and everything, and I mean everything, is done for me. If I need a song I text Llinos or just simply ask her in the studio and it's all sorted. I couldn't imagine being without her.

I've always said that I should be with people who celebrate my being there, not with people who take the mick. As you know, recently my Garden programme has been extended to four hours. I welcomed it, but we needed more content and a total revamp. Together with Llinos, I've managed to do this. The show is constantly evolving and we're currently arranging a start date for Chris' Clinic, a new feature with a registered doctor answering medical questions on air. I'm really looking forward to working with him, although, I'll probably end up asking him questions about me and Gabe. But it's all thanks to Llinos who has liaised to make this segment a reality. I can't imagine her not being there now and rely on her more than I ever envisaged.

It's not just the work that she does, but the way she does it, and the way she treats me. Nothing is too much. She was even my witness at our civil ceremony. She really is the girl of my dreams. I thank my boss every day that he gave me Llinos. I wouldn't want to do it without her.

Strictly fed up

I always loved *Come Dancing* and when *Strictly Come Dancing* came on air, I was chuffed. I've watched several series and talked a lot about it on the radio, discussing the competition in great detail with my listeners – they've been as enthralled too. One night on the radio, someone suggested that I went in for *Strictly Come Dancing* and became a competitor. My immediate reaction was, yes, go for it. But who would want me? – an old faggot! Well, no sooner said, a long-time Garden member and very dear friend, Mark Drane, set up a Facebook page to nominate me for the show.

I wondered would anything come of it. Guess what? Nothing did. I was so surprised. I wasn't really – just being slightly sarcastic! I think I could do it but I don't think I'd ever get the chance. I think I'd have a better chance if I was on an English radio station. I really feel that we're forgotten here in the Principality when it comes to national issues or events. But, you never know, one day they may just call me up and ask me to do it. There's even been talk of gay teams competing. Now that would prove interesting! Watch this space.

Me and sports just don't mix

As you fully well know, I'm not one for sport, certainly not football. It's not my world. When it appears on my telly, I switch it off. Rugby is the same, I can't stand it. Now, this is usually where people say there must be something wrong with me and I can't be Welsh. (More insults for my gallery.)

But, I was particularly moved one evening when listening to a news broadcast before doing my programme. The news story was about a footballer who was gravely ill. The reports didn't sound very optimistic and family, friends and admirers were literally holding their breath. We were even careful about which song we played after the news.

John Hartson. I didn't know him from Adam and I could only send my best wishes for a speedy recovery. I asked for a prayer from the Garden on his behalf. I often say, never underestimate the power of prayer. John regained consciousness, pulled through and has made a remarkable recovery.

I'm trying to remember how we met, but I can't for the life of me. I think I got to know him through the news bulletins throughout his illness. We must have been at a charity bash somewhere along the line. We hit it off fantastically and, on one occasion, when we both attended Mal Pope's Lifetime Achievement Award luncheon, it was like old buddies meeting. I also got the opportunity to meet his dad; they are so alike, it was uncanny.

From then on we were good mates and we've chatted on the phone on numerous occasions: sometimes business issues, other times just idle chitchat. For the first time, and I guess because I usually have no sports' interest, I've realised that coincidences happen regularly. In music and entertainment,

I'd accept these without regard, but for two guys from such different backgrounds and interests, I've found it surprising the number of times we've just missed each other because of various commitments – even down to picking up takeaways from the same establishment within minutes of each other, with the only link being the owner knowing the BBC connection!

John is a true gentleman and is very charitable of this time and knowledge and, more importantly, he is a survivor. I can honestly say that my knowing him has enriched me enormously.

Double trouble

There was a stage production being put on by Karen Struel-White in Swansea with me playing a small cameo part at the end. There were some very good local actors involved, including some old friends. Gabe was in it too, having auditioned without me knowing, and had secured a role. As the production came closer it was suggested that someone else played me, just for the hell of it. But who could honestly play me? My Lord, that would be a task. Someone to portray me! I know I'm larger than life and a bit of a monster, but the ordeal of auditioning for a Chris Needs lookalike started.

Well, eventually, they chose Jonathan Millard from Ebbw Vale. He was sort of the same stamp as me and he could act. He'd have to if he wanted to play me – poor bugger! It must have been strange for him as I was hanging around, and back and forth. So, in effect, he was doing the Chris Needs bit in front of Chris Needs. I bet that was really off-putting. But then, on top of that, he had to act opposite Gabe, my partner. Now there was the test of a lifetime.

Jonathan was actually very good at it. What a clever actor he was to pull that off. He really did me proud and in front of us as an audience as well. Mind you, he must have been shattered leading up to the production as, in addition to attending rehearsals, he shadowed me, picking up my mannerisms and phrases, often calling into the studios to watch me at work late into the night. I often wonder who'd play me in a film of my life story. I reckon this boy Jonathan would be perfect. Well done, Jon.

Chapter 20

October 2013

I'm just taking a look at how my life is at the moment. High or low?

Health – it seems rather hit and miss. My toes are numb and further investigations are imminent. There's a possibility that I have a hiatus hernia and, my God, it's painful. I'm on tablets, which are slightly easing the condition, but I might have to have an operation. My voice is OK but it'll never be the same again as my vocal cords were badly scarred and the healing process seems to have reached a standstill.

Private life – I don't have one. I even gave up my wedding because of work commitments which is why we initially postponed. As I said, I lost the certificate and the time limit almost expired before we were able to reschedule!

Family – nonexistent.

Social life – I don't have one, but I would like one!

Money – people owe me so much money and I don't ever think I'll see it again. You think I'd have learnt by now. There are some right cheeky buggers out there. But no more, they can all sling their hooks. I've just been too generous for far too long.

Holidays – I tried one after the treatment on my throat. It turned out to be not much of a holiday but more of a prison sentence. But then, holidays in general often go wrong for me, so much so that Gabe often says we need to look at having separate holidays!

Me and Gabe – absolutely fine. Never better. I could be more considerate at times, as I'm sure I'm losing the plot. Buster is the most perfect being in my life – nothing but love and more love from him.

Gabe's mam – so very kind to me and expects nothing, fair play.

Me at the BBC – that's about the one big thing which keeps me from going off my head. It helped with my recovery when I was ill. But it can also be an intense place to work. I have to be right at all times, I can't let my guard down.

The gay thing – I wish I wasn't gay in south Wales. It's a nightmare. I'm still called names to this day. And there's me thinking it was an offence to call anyone a derogatory name. I must be mistaken.

Where to live? – if I move again it's Spain, Spain and more Spain – end of. Unless it's Gibraltar!

Shopping – when I go shopping with a friend I always tell them, just as I enter the shop, here's my smile, just in case someone says that Chris Needs is a miserable bugger.

Will I continue to call people flower and angel? – yes, you bet, even though someone wrote in and said they didn't like me saying flower all of the time. My answer to them is tough cheese, flower!

My hair – I'll never ever give up straightening my hair till the day I die. If I die and there's some hair product left, I'll leave it all to Carole Rees Jones!

My eyes – I'm tempted to have laser treatment on my eyes as I'm finding glasses bloody hard work.

Shoes – I'll always wear pointy ones. They're fab.

Incidentally, as it's fresh in my mind: as I was walking to the Rolling Mill today for a bit of Sunday lunch, three drunk lads walked towards me and Gabe, and one started shouting my name and could he have a photo? I just laughed. Then, they went into our shop where Louise was serving and one of them dropped his trousers. I was very put out when she told me. I was very upset I bloody missed that one. And apparently, it was worth staring at! Never mind, we've got it on security tape. Perhaps he'd like it on Facebook?

I used to think that people were wonderful until they dirtied on me but, now, I think that people are sods till they prove themselves to me (well some, anyway).

My celebrity friends – they mean the world to me. We understand each other so well. I'll always try to help them, like they've been so good to me.

Garden members – are always a reminder of the success of the programme. My God, I've met some wonderful people through the Garden: politicians, royalty, aristocracy, doctors, legends, superstars and, of course, the nice folk who are proud Garden members. I've been a lucky boy in some ways: I've always been in work, doing a job that I love. It's not a job though, it's a vocation.

Do I want a birthday party for my 60th? I've thought and thought about this one, and I've decided to do exactly what I want. I don't want a party after all. I just want to be with Gabe and Buster. Maybe have a tea party with Gabe's family. But I'd like to see a rip-roaring opera or a drag show!

Any regrets? YES, bloody loads!

I wish I hadn't sold my place in Gibraltar. I wish I hadn't trusted people so much. I wish I hadn't taken those bloody tablets that specialist gave me. I wish I'd sold all the houses and just kept one like normal people. I wish I'd had animals years ago. I wish I could have done more for my mother. I wish I wasn't gay in Wales (torture). I wish I'd not smoked. I wish I'd fathered a child when I was 18 – I'd have had to be hypnotized though! I wish I was thicker skinned. I wish I was taller. I wish I had a family. I wish I had the guts to name that man who abused me as a child, but I'm frightened I'd ruin some people's lives. (Ha, ha, me thinking of others again. Stuff me! As long as everybody else is OK.) I suppose if I lived abroad the scars and bitterness would still be there. What am I to do?

I wish my boss would say to me, "Chris, do your programme from Spain."

I've got my godson Sam and I suppose as he gets older, he'll be taking me out in the car for a trip. Blink, and the time is gone. He's wonderful.

A welcome phone call

Sue Lambert had always been a big part of my life but we sort of drifted apart a couple of years ago. I'd thought about her off and on over the years and promised myself I'd get in touch but never got around to it. I suppose with the numerous changes of address (mainly on my part) and various new telephone numbers, it was going to be more of tracking her down. This was obviously going to take time, so I kept putting it off.

Imagine my surprise and delight when she contacted me last night at the studio. I was immediately filled with joy. She was the sister I'd never had. She practically lived in my house in the 1970s and we literally made music wherever we went. We were like the dynamic duo; her singing and me on the keyboards. Now remember, there were no backing tracks in those days, just the club organist.

The backing in those days was very hit and miss and, most of the time, it sounded like there was a cat running up and down the keyboards. So, when Sue and me went out to the clubs together, and with us singing duets as well – the world stood still!

My mother and father adored her and were waiting for me to come home and say that we were going to be married. Of course, that was never going to be! When we went to Belgium to visit my father's brother, Sue would organise everything and she'd even carry the cases. In fact, we went everywhere together. Automatically, my mother put a dinner away for her and Sue loved being up in Cwmafan back then, in the early 1970s. We would rehearse songs every day and our house in Cwmafan was always filled with music and show business people.

The same applied to Sue's home in Swansea. Her mother

treated me like another son; in fact, she called me son when she spoke to me.

Sue and me worked with Bonnie Tyler and her sister Avis on a regular basis, mainly in the Townsman Club in Swansea and the Sandman Club in Aberafan.

These were the days when we worked with Aquarius. It was all so good back then.

I don't know to this day why we didn't see each other of late, but it was fortunate that I bumped into Sue's mother Sylvia recently in the Dunvant Club in Swansea. I didn't recognise her at first but when I finally realised who she was, I was chuffed and felt like a good cry. I told Sylvia that I was desperate to see Sue again and she took my mobile number.

When Sue called it was as if it was only yesterday that we'd last seen each other and immediately I knew that everything was all right. We've yet to meet up but I'm looking forward immensely to that day. She mentioned that she'd heard that I'd been ill and that she hadn't been too well herself – and asked me was I happy?

That threw me a bit. I looked back over my life, over the past 20-odd years, over the last three, and I told her "some days". And Sue replied, "That's how it is love, that's how it is."

10 October 2013 – Super Thursday

Today's the day that publishers release the titles of the books they hope will be bestsellers at Christmas. But I've still loads more to say…

I knew it was going to be a busy day and, believe you me, it was. I was feeling quite unwell with chest pains and, after seeing a specialist privately, he felt that it was more of an ulcer/reflux problem than angina, which my father died of.

So off me and Gabe go; him driving, and me holding my chest, not to mention my feet as well. We arrived at Albany Road Post Office in Roath, Cardiff, where they were enjoying a big relaunch and rebranding of the store, and very nice it was too. I met lots of Garden members; it was so nice to meet up again. It was fun to share the banter over the microphone and everybody seemed pleased to see me.

I really love personal appearances and getting to meet everyone face to face. It's great also to put faces to the voices that ring me up on the radio show. The bonus for me and Gabe was meeting up with Ray Griffiths, a former policeman from Gwent. He'd arranged this appearance for me and I was really pleased to receive a donation to help towards the Chris Needs Hospital Appeal. We are a registered charity supporting hospitals and healthcare organisations solely based in Wales who need assistance towards aids or appliances for patients to assist with their recovery and rehabilitation. The last time we were together we'd been invited to a police HQ open day at Pontypool a few years back. We'd taken the motor home, a few trestle tables and, together with Countess Christine and Lady Catherine, we sold practically half the stock of the charity shop.

Later we went off to Cardiff Castle. This is where Guide Dogs for the Blind were holding a demonstration and advice day. It was Guide Dog week and I was excited. It might have been bright and sunny but, in the shade, it was so cold. There was a large crowd of dog lovers assembled and I met up with some more of my listeners.

The demonstrator was Andrew and he explained first of all that this was not an 'animal charity'. The association had been formed for those with major vision problems and the dogs were an aid that blind people used to get about, and to maintain and improve their independence. The dogs, without the harness, were merely dogs. But, once the harness was on, they were working dogs, guide dogs. Andrew's dog, Delphi, was gorgeous and understood instructions and acted accordingly, except when he knew that there was danger ahead. That's when his training mode kicked in. Delphi stopped when there was an obstacle and, when being told to move on, he wouldn't budge until he'd assessed the situation and made the necessary decision to divert. He was incredible. I was so impressed and wondered what I'd have done if I was put in that situation.

My turn came – I was blindfolded and the harness was put in my hand. I held Delphi and he made me feel safe immediately. Andrew is sighted and, as he talked, Delphi took me around the course, with Andrew altering the obstacles to make it more challenging. I learnt that guide dogs are constantly assessing when they are at work and usually looking several yards ahead for problems they and their owners may come across.

Andrew also mentioned the importance of the first year in a puppy's life and how the association rely on puppy walkers fostering a puppy until their training starts. I hope Gabe wasn't listening too intensely!

I was bowled over with what was happening. After taking my blindfold off, there was a tremendous round of applause and I felt good. I'd done it. I was introduced to many blind people and their dogs and the association's officials. I was really chuffed. I'm so lucky to be asked to do different things, all because I'm on the radio and TV. And here's another good cause for me to support. I intend to donate the proceeds of a stage show to a guide dog association. I'd also like to involve myself more with the practical side of guide dogs. Have I opened a can of worms? I think so, and I'm glad I have.

This is also the day that I've decided that me and Gabe are better off living in Cardiff than in Cwmafan, simply because the travelling is too much and we need some time for ourselves. I'm finding the trip back to Port Talbot from Cardiff every night a big strain. So, we've decided to put more staff in the shop and Gabe and me can have a bit of a life. I'll still have contact with Cwmafan, but none of the late-night travelling, especially with winter heading towards us.

I'm looking forward to a slightly easier life and doing nicer things. Regarding my health, it's not that clever. Between my throat and my poor diabetic legs, I don't know. But at the end of the day, do I make a song and dance of things? Do I hell? (JOKE)

As for me and how I feel right now – my health is a problem. I don't plan on having a ten-year savings plan to be honest. But I'm making sure that Gabe is OK. I won't be leaving him anything really. I'll be signing it all over to him before I pop my clogs so then I can rest in peace and nobody can contest anything. What's mine is all Gabe's. Put it this way, if Gabe needed a kidney, he could have the two of mine. But, in the meantime, as I've said before, we both need to start enjoying ourselves.

In conclusion
by Gabe Cameron

DID YOU HONESTLY think Chris was going to have the last word? Oh please, he's still supposed to be resting his voice and taking it easy. Although far from well, I guess these last few months have brought about the turnaround everyone was waiting for. But Chris, at times, seems to think he's invincible and tries to accomplish tasks to a level that he was at before he became ill. It's true when he says we both need to live a little before it's too late.

This has been a most difficult typescript to edit and more time consuming than even I imagined. Due to Chris' moods and depression, and not just in the early days of his ill health, the entries were often duplicated. Sometimes a daily diary, then other entries compiled into the journal on a more ad hoc basis. To have left them in, the repetitive content would have shown the extent of his depressive moods and would have been a harrowing read, too. I've tried to balance out his feelings in battling his illness alongside memories of his life and normal day-to-day issues.

He continues to credit me for him still being about today, but I can only accept half of the praise. I honestly believe it's Buster which has kept him going. The love, affection and attention that Buster gave Chris when I wasn't about was astounding and, in return, Chris had to get up and feed him, let him out and take him for short walks in my absence. Buster may have been my dog but he is Chris' buddy and companion, and whines just as much for Chris when he's not about as he does for me.

Long-time listeners will recall that Chris didn't like pets at all, didn't like dogs in particular and, true to what he's said, offered me money to pass Buster on to someone else. I guess my stubbornness paid off, and to Chris' advantage as it turned out.

Chris wasn't always so anti-animal. When he first moved to Cardiff he adopted a tomcat called Willie. You may have tuned in to hear callers enquiring about Chris' big fat Willie on both his independent show and when he transferred to BBC Radio Wales. Willie used to allow all the strays in to share his food and, at one time, Chris shared his home with nine cats – the most infamous, of course, Delyth Du. But one by one, they moved on leaving Willie to grow old and alone.

When Willie died, it was our friend Bethan, Ryan Davies's daughter, who took him to the vets. Chris was too upset to take him, fearing the worst... and I collected him. We buried him in the garden in Cwmafan, along with his favourite blanket, toys and photos of us. A simple ceremony, and Chris vowed never to have another pet as it was too upsetting and also restrictive if we wanted to go away.

The year before Chris was taken ill, I wasn't in good health myself and took quite some time off work. It gave me a chance to re-evaluate my own life at that time, to re-establish contact with old friends, to return to painting etc. We spent practically the whole year in Porthcawl. I loved the privacy that the caravan at Trecco Bay gave us. I could work for hours in the garden and escape from everyone for days at a time. It was during this period that I started to think again about having a dog.

Chris, I think, was a little frightened of them, having been once targeted by a nasty, nipping Chow. On the other hand, I was terrorised by a Jack Russell and her puppy as a child. My grandparents' house was at the far end of a cul-de-sac. I swear these dogs would lay in wait, watching me make my way up the road until I'd passed all paths with easy, unlockable gates. I used to clamber on to garden walls as soon as I heard them yapping towards me and proceed to my grandparents' house like an act from Barnum's Circus – all the time these damn dogs would be jumping up to try and make me lose my balance.

But I wanted a dog. We had looked after Harry, Chris' godson Sam's dog, a number of times when the family were off on holiday. Friends advised that I really should consider taking in a rescue dog as they needed love and attention more than most. I agreed too, but when I learnt that Buster, barely six months old, was not settling in with his new family and was back at the kennels awaiting new owners, I knew he needed rescuing too. Well, it was Chris' own fault – he told me of Buster's plight!

When we met at the kennels we immediately bonded. All the way home, he sat on my lap while I drove, and all the rules I made in the first few weeks, i.e. no begging from the table, no climbing up on furniture, no access into the bedroom... were all broken when Chris finally bonded with Buster!

Well, we wouldn't be without him now. And, I firmly believe that we wouldn't have Chris either if it wasn't for Buster, not just me.

Also from Y Lolfa:

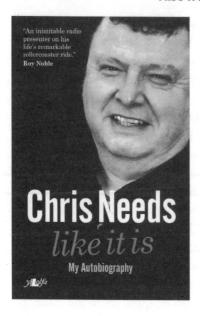

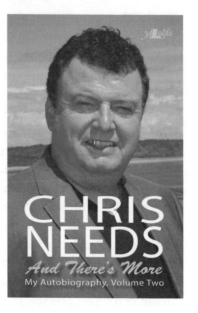

Highs and Lows is just one of a whole range of publications from Y Lolfa. For a full list of books currently in print, send now for your free copy of our new full-colour catalogue. Or simply surf into our website

www.ylolfa.com

for secure on-line ordering.

Talybont Ceredigion Cymru SY24 5HE
e-mail ylolfa@ylolfa.com
website www.ylolfa.com
phone (01970) 832 304
fax 832 782